PAGES FROM THE DIARY OF A SMALL TOWN GIRL

PRAGYA

© **Pragya 2022**

All rights reserved

All rights reserved by author. No part of this publication may be reproduced, stored in a retrieval system or transmitted in any form or by any means, electronic, mechanical, photocopying, recording or otherwise, without the prior permission of the author.

Although every precaution has been taken to verify the accuracy of the information contained herein, the author and publisher assume no responsibility for any errors or omissions. No liability is assumed for damages that may result from the use of information contained within.

First Published in January 2022

ISBN: 978-93-5472-954-6

BLUEROSE PUBLISHERS

www.bluerosepublishers.com
info@bluerosepublishers.com
+91 8882 898 898

Cover Design:
Debjani Hazarika

Typographic Design:
Namrata Saini

Distributed by: BlueRose, Amazon, Flipkart

A Child, A Woman & The phoenix—
"Page's from the diary of a small town girl".

Preface

The sole reason of writing this book is not only to bring forth the trials and tribulations of a vulnerable woman who could not raise her voice against everything that befell her, but to say the unsaid things which can be eye opener to many. I know I am an ordinary woman to tell my story and thus I urge my readers to try and understand that in doing so I have a purpose. I wish some things had never happened and also that I should have been strong enough to resist the few occurrences. However, it does not make sense in regretting anything now but I wish that in narrating my personal experience would make many of us realize that it's very important to pay heed to certain issues beforehand to avoid anything that may affect anyone's mental and physical well being. In due course I struggled, survived and learnt lessons and have been fortunate enough to gather confidence to move on. Now I wish never to shy away from my responsibilities towards myself, my children, my near and dear ones and to the society. Hope this extraordinary story of an ordinary woman can become a way to create some awareness in us.

About the author:

The author faced a lot in her life but managed to overcome all those to become a successful model who represented the country in the Mrs. Universe contest. She is a former Mrs. India winner and is also a successful entrepreneur. She actively participates in humanitarian activities across Assam and focuses on helping underprivileged children. Furthermore, she is raising two children of her own, including a daughter, and wants her to live in a safer society in the future. Finally, it takes courage, in a conservative society, to bear open the most difficult moments of one's life, and the author is willing to do that in order to serve the society.

Contents

Introduction 1

22/03/2020 (during the pandemic time) 4

Motto: 8

The 1st incident - Twilight Hide and Seek 10

The 2nd Instance (Something that happened
many times over) 13

3rd Incident – Guests at home. 18

4th Incident - Flood like Blood 22

5th Incident – Fresh Peanuts 27

6th Incident – Dharma 31

7th Incident– An educated teacher 36

8th Incident – Bihu Function 41

More reasons and situations 46

Important and unacceptable behavior 48

The poor, the destitute, and the orphans 53

The after effects of abuse 57

After Marriage 60

Introduction

I have tried very hard to obliterate many past memories, especially those from my childhood through visits to therapists, psychiatrists and meditation. I suppose, I have been successful to a large extent, however, I still have my doubts, especially during the times when the mind is disturbed. I know for a fact that it is not easy to erase memories; especially the ones which have had a profound effect on my life. Despite knowing it, there are times when I break down and feel shattered. And this very feeling of disgust, dismay and lack of self love leads to me to not just hurt myself, but also has an adverse effect on my family and their peace of mind and happiness, which also led to broken relationships. Some of which may never be fixed no matter what the amends. Arguments with my parents, ego clashes with my brother, and a general contempt for the masculine gender has led to much bitterness and at times, much resentment too. Although most of my friends and near ones joke that I refuse to take my blinds off, see only what I want to see and not give others the benefit of doubt. I know deep within that they are complaining and hate the fact that I behave like a race horse; focused only on my point of view. I'm filled with so much doubt and contempt for males that there are times I fear leaving my daughter alone even with the very man who helped me bring my child into this world. There are instances, where without any warning, I snatch her away from my husband; her father, and hold her tight against my chest. Then there are the lectures on moral values and how to treat women that I dole out to my son endlessly just because I believe that children should have a strict and moral upbringing and not be allowed to make mistakes. It is, after all, my firm belief that childhood is when the foundations should be built.

I've had many nightmares; ones where I find myself being smothered, even suffocated. No matter how hard I try, I just can't seem to lift myself up and get out of bed. I wake up, drenched in cold sweat, shaking and in shock. My childhood memories are still fresh; like they happened just yesterday. It's almost as if these memories follow me around everywhere I go, every person I meet and everything I see. I feel just like that little girl who gets her periods for the first time; scared and dirty. It's as though that putrid smell of the first period is following me around. I never realized when I lost my virginity, and I suppose I'll never understand why. This is what those terms "Child Abuse" means to me now.

I grew up learning how to nurture, respect and value relationships. That's why I kept quiet for 25 years of my life; just for the reason that the relationships with the ones I love aren't broken, and so that I don't appear to be a rebel going against the norms of the society that I lived in. And then there was always the fear; the fear of being ridiculed, the fear of being criticized, and maybe even ostracized from that society. And then just like a volcano or an earth shattering quake, or like the lid taken off a hot pressure cooker, I exploded one day. This was just after my little girl was born; the year, 2013. I was scared; scared that if I stayed silent any longer, my little girl would have to suffer the same trauma and consequences that I have had to live with all my life. I was scared that that innocent little girl would also have to bear it all just the way I did and pretend to live a normal life even though there would be nothing normal about it. For the first time in my life, I decided to break my silence and narrated my ordeals to my husband before I did to my mother. I still remember that year 2013 very vividly and all that we had to go through. Yes, although I felt like a huge boulder had been lifted off my chest, relieved, yet, deep within I felt that there was still something left undone, incomplete.

22/03/2020
(during the pandemic time)

It's bed time and Morom, my sweet little angel wants me to read her a bedtime story. She just loves listening to stories while she drops off to sleep. I use these bedtime storytelling sessions as an excuse to bring up some of my childhood experiences. Sometimes, I fictionalize some of my own incidents or those of the others who've had similar experiences as I have. But tonight is different. My little one asks "Ma, have you ever seen a fairy"? Without batting an eye-lid, I respond, "No I haven't, but I have seen the devil. They appear whenever you aren't aware and they can attack you and hurt you very bad. And the worst part is that they look just like us, but are very bad and they use that to do many bad things that can harm you for life." And after that, for really late into the night, I sat with the 7 year old little girl and started to explain to her how she needs to be aware of her body and how she needs to protect herself and her body from others. I went into details of how her body was hers alone and how no one else has the right to touch her without her permission, how some people are attracted to some parts of her body and how people who try to touch her are bad people. I explained all this with a lot of care and it seems she understood what I was trying to tell her and I believe that the decision I took that night was absolutely the right one. And the other right decision that I took that night was to also explain how the devil comes into your life, and how society needs to be made aware was also absolutely right. And that's when I decided to pen my story starting from my childhood.

By narrating my own personal and sensitive stories, through this book, I wish to highlight the problems faced by many children who have been victim of abuse at some point or the other. Despite living with their biological parents, getting all the love and attention that a child is supposed to get, why is it that they always feel alone? Why do they feel like they have lost everyone despite having people around them? Why can't the parents and loved ones protect the innocent child from such abuse?

Perhaps those innocent ones assumed that they would become the laughing stock, or they would be reprimanded by their elders, beaten even, or that they would be socially shamed and all doors shall closed to them forever. And perhaps, after such incidents, they had lost trust in all the people around them. And by the time they realized what was happening, they had already crossed that phase in life. There are many even today who live their lives in shame, in fear and no way to express them and with no one that they think they can trust. Why is it like that? Why is it that even in the 21st century where we talk about freedom and liberation of women can they not live free and fearless lives?

I don't wish to reveal the identities of the people because of whom I've had to write this book. That is not my intention at all. It isn't another "Me Too" story. What I want to highlight is my sadness, my turmoil behind every smile, every laugh, and every moment of happiness. What I'm looking for is that everyone is aware so that their children's futures are bright and so that the children may have fond memories of their childhood. I am the mother of two children, which helps me understand what every mother goes through; their fears and their trials. I also understand well that what some of the children who have or are suffering what I suffered must be going through. This also extends to some men too who have suffered such abuse as little boys.

I wish to make a request to the society at large through this autobiography. I wish that everyone opens their eyes and not remain blind. I want to showcase the sadness and the painful stories that are hidden behind the smiles of many. I'm not looking for sympathy or to make any kind of profit through this memoir and the stories, but what I really want is for people to be aware and to be able to protect their children from falling prey to abuse so that they are able to fully enjoy their childhood and grow up to be beautiful and caring individuals. I have been blessed with two lovely children, which helps me understand the fears that only a mother would know. Memories from my childhood also help me understand and empathize those who have suffered similar abuse as children. What it is like to live life with those memories, the trauma of suffering silently, the constant irritations and nagging fears. Through these true stories, I make an earnest request to all the mothers to be aware and responsible, and also to the society at large to create a healthy and safe environment for our children to grow up in. Children are delicate, fragile and their minds are innocent. No one has the right to take that away from them. No one has the right to abuse them in any way. I further request through this book to act humane and allow children to enjoy their childhood. Let them carry with them pleasant memories from their childhood. Offer them a safe and secure environment to grow and flourish. Unless we are alert and create that sense of awareness, your own children may have to face the devil of abuse; and you may have the next victim in your own home and you might never even come to know about it.

Motto:

The main idea behind my writing this book is not to lay any kind of allegations on anyone's kind of parenting. Neither is it my intention to deride the current system of education. And further away is my intention to malign any form of societal norms. I only wish to highlight how, even in this modern and so called civilized and evolved world, close to 50% of the children are abused. And I speak not just about sexual abuse; but also include mental, physical and neglect. What I'm trying to say is that any form of pain or hurt caused to a child can be considered as abuse. If we as parents, young adults or even as the elderly do not become aware and take corrective action, the cycle of child abuse, criminal behavior, victim and the shattered will continue.

I haven't illustrated my own horrendous experiences in this book to make them topics of discussions and entertainment. I do not wish that this becomes just another coffee table book; neither do I wish that it gets relegated to the deepest, darkest corner of your shelf. The intention behind this book is to awaken you to the fact that children do suffer and for you to try and make use of this book to try and understand your children and also for you to try and help protect them from the evil lurking behind every corner, every person.

I also wish for education departments, educators, and schools; especially across this country, to try and add a system of learning across all institutes to enable these innocent little beings better protect themselves not just from sexual abuse, but also from any other forms of abuse.

The 1st incident - Twilight Hide and Seek

I normally don't forget things. However, it is possible that over time, some memories may get distorted or lost.

I must have been just about 5 or 6 years old. I didn't leave home expecting to come face to face with the devil himself in human form that day. I didn't expect that someone would want to taste my fresh meat that day.

I am the middle child. However, I don't clearly remember if my younger sister was born then. As far as I can remember, that day I had gone to play in the field in front of my uncle's house with a few of my friends. My elder brother was in the local club nearby, hanging out with his friends. It was turning dark and all of my friends returned home. There was an elderly boy who I somewhat knew, but was not very familiar with, approached me. The place where I was raised wasn't very populated and almost everybody in the area recognized one another even if they didn't know each other well enough. And that's how I knew him too; not closely, but just that he lived in the same area and that he had a younger sister who danced very well. Like I mentioned earlier, it is not my interest to reveal anyone's identity through this book, hence I would like to withhold the name of that person.

Even though it had turned quite dark, I did recognize him from being from the same area as ours. He approached me and we sat on the grass and started chatting. He sat with his legs straight and in a manspread and made me sit in the empty space between his legs. He made sure that he sat in a way where I had my back to him. After a while, I felt a subtle touch near my hips, like he was looking for something on my body. Even though I was young, I knew that there was something wrong that he was doing to me. It just didn't feel right. When I tried to move away, he closed his legs around me and locked me in between his legs. I was scared and in that fright I started to scream out to by brother hoping that he could hear me. That's when this person let me go, got up quickly, scolded me for screaming unnecessarily and walked away.

Maybe because I was still very young and innocent, but I soon forgot about the incident. Or maybe I didn't thoroughly understand the magnitude of the incident. Even today I fail to understand exactly why I didn't say anything about this to my mother. All I remember is that from that day onwards, I just couldn't stand the sight of that person, although I would greet him only when occasion demanded. As time went by, and I was older I realized that what this person had done to me that day wasn't really a very good thing and that his intentions weren't at all morally acceptable. I also noticed that this person had some kind of a skin ailment that was very visible. One day when I was standing with my mother near the gate in the courtyard, he happened to pass by. As a sign of recognition, he waved a greeting to my mother and continued down the road. After he crossed, I asked my mother why his skin was the way it was. I still remember what my mother said. "He must have done some really bad things. I've heard that he isn't a very good person." Maybe he really did some really unacceptable things and maybe my mother knew about some of those things. Whatever, the case, deep within, I was very happy that he had that skin ailment. I'm sure he deserved it.

*Why did that have to happen to me? Why couldn't that person control his appetite and not abuse me? Maybe I didn't understand exactly what that was all about or maybe I lacked the knowledge because of my tender age. It could be because my mother didn't explain things to me the way I did to my little one about how the devil can also appear in a human avatar. It's also possible that my mother innocently never thought about all of these, or couldn't even fathom the idea of anyone harming a sweet, innocent girl like that. *

The 2nd Instance
(Something that happened many times over)

The town that I grew up in wasn't a very large one. You can safely say that it was a very small town and except for the basic essentials, it was primarily undeveloped. Our house was a little far away from the heart of the town but more accessible from the main college area. Since our house was conveniently located for people from the rural areas that came to study in the college, my father decided to rent a portion of our house out for some additional income. I met a lot of people in my childhood, especially students and mostly boys that came to live in our house.

I don't wish to reveal the name, but I remember I that I used to call him uncle. I don't exactly remember how long he stayed at our rented house, but I remember seeing him from a very young age. When I came to an age of understanding, I got to know that he was from the same village as my grandmother and that we shared an extended family relationship. Younger Uncle, or "Khura" in Assamese is what I used to call him. He came to study at the college and once he completed his education, stayed behind to help out at one of his relatives' stores. My father mostly stayed away owing to his job and my mother single handedly raised the three of us. Khura was a big help and he used to revere my mother. Eventually, he became like a very well trusted family member to us. He could come and go as he pleased and whenever my mother had to step out for some work, we would be left under his care. In short, he was exactly like another member of our family. I would always feel very uneasy around him. But maybe I couldn't understand why because of my age.

I would often accompany my mother to the main town, especially when she went shopping for groceries. She would always visit that Khura at the store and leave me behind in his care while she went shopping for meats and fish. Perhaps she didn't like to take me to the fish or the poultry market because it wasn't very clean or hygienic.

Once when she went to the market, as usual, she left me behind at the store with this Khura. He offered me toffees and many other eatables from the shop. I still remember that day as though it was yesterday because that was the first time that this Khura's devilish avatar came into being. I noticed that he was reading a book. After a while, he asked me to join him in reading and made me sit next to him. He started showing me some of the pictures in the book and started to explain the meaning of what was written in the book. I realized that the things he was showing me weren't really meant for children. It seemed more like things that were meant for adults. It was the kind of scenes where my mother would turn off the TV or send me off to bring something just when they came on. I understood that this was sex related material. He used that open book to cover himself, caught my hand and forced it down his trousers while he pushed his other hand under my frock and tried to fiddle with my privates. I was saved that day because a customer suddenly entered the store and the Khura got busy serving the customer. After the customer left, the Khura came and tried to explain things to me. He also said, "Don't tell anyone about this because people will laugh at you and your mother will also scold you." I was genuinely scared and in that fright I didn't speak a word of it to anyone, including my mother.

From that day on, he started behaving extra caring towards me. He would bring me chocolates or at times give me Rs.10/-. And every time he gave me anything he would ask me if I told anyone about the incident and would also threaten me. Not only that. One day I was in the kitchen and he had brought some things from the market. My mother was not at home. Seizing the opportunity, he tried to strike a deal with me. He said that if I did exactly as he said, he would always bring me tasty snacks and eatables from the market and that I could have whatever I wanted from the store. In short, he was bartering with me for sexual favors.

He would keep pestering me like that many times. But when I realized what he was exactly after, I stopped talking to him altogether and started to avoid him. I would always look for excuses to not come face to face with him. After a while, his younger sister came to live with him and he stopped pestering me. It's possible that his advances stopped because I was very friendly with his sister and maybe that's what got him scared.

*No one can be trusted, especially when it comes to a relation between a male and a female. I suppose that is what I learnt from this person: never trust a man. Why did this happen? Maybe my parents gave him the freedom thinking that he was trustable and that he could be of some help to the house. And that's why they also gave him that freedom. Maybe this is the price that I had to pay for his help. Just for the sake of a little extra income, I wasn't safe in my own home. Maybe my parents didn't realize that keeping male students in a house when there's a girl child is like letting a tiger loose in front of a deer.

Since my dad was mostly away, my mother had to take the burden of running and maintaining the entire household. And that's why she was unable to monitor all activities very closely. Or is it that that Khura was actually a real bad person? Or is it just that men just can't keep their sexual greed under control? However, isn't it unacceptable to offer children money, just so that they don't develop a greed for material things? Maybe that's why I didn't say a word; because I'd get my pocket money and all the other things that I wanted; something that my parents never noticed. *

3rd Incident – Guests at home.

I suppose I was about 8 or 9 years old at the time, definitely not more than 10, and it was around the same year when the 2nd incident took place. It was also the time when our house was being renovated. An extra bed was put up in the living room for guests and my mother and little sister slept in my room. Given the age, there may be some things that I have difficulty recollecting, yet I'll try and explain all that I remember.

There was a guest that arrived one day and he decided to stay over for a while. He was related to my mother through her extended family, and we used to call him "Nisadeu". It's time I gave you a slight background about myself. I am from the Ahom community of Assam and in our language a mother's elder brother is addressed as "Nisadeu".

Let me also give you a brief description of what my family is like. My parents are very simple people who live a very simple life. They are absolutely trusting and think that people never actually mean any harm. I remember during my days in the parental house, they would welcome anyone from their village to stay over for any length of time with open arms. Anyone who came visiting for whatever purpose was always made to feel at home and my parents would go out of their way to extend their hospitality; even if the guest arrived unannounced. I noticed that ever since my childhood. Not only that, my father would also like to help people who had completed a jail term; there was a time when my father was posted as the in-charge of Dibrugarh Central Jail. My father would help the prisoners who had served their time. He would send them off to work at my grandmother's fields, help them with money to reach their own homes, and at times even bring them to stay with us at our home. In fact, I remember sitting down to meals with many different criminals.

Given my parent's easy going and hospitable nature, people would love being guests at our home. The Nisadeu who had come to stay that day was not just related to my mother, but also someone who my dad knew well enough. He was slightly older than my father; maybe about 55 years of age. He also had a very charming personality and he engaged us kids very nicely with his stories.

Because Nisadeu was the guest for the night, dinner was an exquisite affair with many different delicious dishes. We Ahoms usually consume a beer made of fermented rice during the festivals and special occasions. And since we had a special guest, it was time to bring out the rice beer. After a lot of fun and a delicious dinner, we headed off to bed. Nisadeu asked me to sleep with him and tempted me by saying that he would narrate a story.

In retrospect, it seems that the story was just a web and the main fiend in that story was Nisadeu himself. I don't remember the exact sequence of events that followed, but all I remember distinctly is that just as I was half asleep, I could feel that someone was tugging at my panties and I could feel a hand trying to grope my privates. I squiggled around a bit and managed to lift my panties back up. However, when I woke up again towards the middle of the night, I found that my panties had been taken off again and I could actually feel the body of that middle aged man trying desperately to satiate his hunger on my puny little body.

I was terrified. In my innocent little mind I thought it was some kind of a ghost that was touching me in the middle of the night. I darted out of that bed and rushed to where my mother was sleeping. But I was too terrified to say anything to her. She never once asked me why I came away from that room and I never bothered telling her either. Maybe she never realized that something else may be wrong in that deep sleep of hers. Or maybe she didn't think anything was amiss and never gave it a second thought considering that I was a little girl and almost all little girls seek out their mothers at night anyway.

From what I remember, Nisadeu was all packed and ready to leave early next morning even before I had woken up. The last thing that I remember from that day is that he came inside to call out to us and I pretended to be fast asleep. Except for just another time in the future, I don't think I ever met him ever again.

*What I would like to know however is that, whose fault was it really? Was it the alcohol that made him lose control or was it his inherent nature? Is it that he did not understand the feelings of a girl even though he was a father to a daughter himself? Or was I at fault for agreeing to share the bed with him? Or was it my mother's fault for not warning us to get too close to him physically? Could it be that guests shouldn't be allowed to stay over or is it really possible that relationships don't really have any value whatsoever? *

4th Incident - Flood like Blood

Even today, there's a special place in the heart for the maternal grandparents' house. Almost every Indian child has a special kind of attraction towards their maternal uncles. In the same way, I was always the happiest whenever I got the opportunity to go to my maternal grandparents' house. We did not have the Bogibeel bridge then, and a visit to my grandparents meant traversing across the mighty Brahmaputra for 8 hours on a ferry to get to the other side because Enaido; meaning grandmother in our culture, lived across on the other bank of the river in Lakhimpur. I really enjoyed the ride across the Brahmaputra. It had a lot more water than it has today. The sight of big fish surfacing, river dolphins playing and jumping in the water mesmerized me.

I don't remember the exact year. What I do remember however, was that it was the summer vacations. I don't even remember who I went with, but all I know is that we stayed there for a very long time. Mainly because, by the time we reached, the floods had hit and the ferry services had been stopped. We were locked in by water on all sides. Even today, Lakhimpur is known in Assam for the floods; especially during the monsoon season.

That was the first time in my life when I had experienced floods of such a major magnitude. I still remember, the house had a large open space in front of it and it had filled up completely. We would sit on the verandah on stools and catch fish. And we did catch a lot of fish; in fact, some of them would swim right up to us to be caught. I still remember that we would boat around the place to see how many areas had been inundated. I also saw and rode boats made of banana stalks for the first time in my life that year. My mother's elder brother's kids- my cousins, were almost around the same age as me and we would venture out together to explore the area. Once we even tried to navigate a boat ourselves without any help and fell into the water. We had to wade through the water to get back up and by the time we got onto dry earth, our legs were full of leech. I still remember how we cried in pain and fright; well! more in fright, at the sight of those huge black creatures stuck to our legs and refusing to let go. Those were fun days.

When I was there, I accompanied Enaideu to a gathering at a neighbor's house one evening. It got dark by the time we came home and there was also a slight drizzle. I clung on to Enaideu and we reached home by the light of her torch. Now, my mother had 3 brothers out of which the youngest one was everyone's favorite. When we reached home we got to know that the youngest son, my uncle, was running a fever. My grandmother was a little worried and since she didn't want him to be all alone, she asked me to sleep with him for the night. I didn't see any problem there because I would generally sleep with him whenever I visited. Also, I really enjoyed his company since, he being the youngest he would mostly join us in having fun.

He had never behaved badly or in any untoward way with me. In fact, he also called me by a certain name very affectionately; a name that I detest and hate anyone calling me by today. I freshened up, changed into my nightdress and went to sleep with my favorite uncle. I remember that his part of the house was slightly away from the main house and was somewhat isolated. It also didn't have any electricity. I reached there by the lamp of a torch. The moment I climbed into bed, I gave him a tight hug and went to sleep holding him. I still remember how warm he was because of the fever. We chatted for a little while and I must have dropped off while we were still talking. It must have been around midnight. I woke with a start and felt my uncle's warm body on top of me and trying to enter my tiny little vagina. I acted as though I was still sleepy and put my panties back on in my sleep. My uncle must have assumed that whatever I did, I must have been doing in my sleep and was not really aware of what was going on. However, my past experience at home with the middle aged man had taught me a lesson and I stayed alert although I pretended to be asleep. In actuality, I couldn't sleep the whole night out of fear. My uncle kept calling out to me to see if I was really asleep and I continued to pretend that I was. I'd keep pretending that my sleep was being disturbed and slowly wriggled out of his clutches and assumed a safer sleeping position. I was in tremendous pain and even today, when I think about it, I shudder. I was scared and I could do nothing about it. As a child, I was always scared of ghosts. Since the room was pitch dark and as my uncle's place was slightly isolated and away from the main house, I couldn't even get up and run and sleep with my grandmother. I kept thinking about getting up and running away from his place, but I just couldn't bring myself to do it. I just wasn't able to figure out what I needed to do.

The moment it was daybreak and there was some sunlight, I got up and went to my grandmother's room. When I came face to face with my uncle much later in the day, he joked with everyone that I was blabbering in my sleep. He tried to prove to everyone that I was acting very foolish in my sleep. There was a devilish fiend hiding behind his laughter that day. Till this day I wonder how could he even do something like that and not feel any remorse. From that day on, even though I maintained a sense of cordiality with him, I refused to sleep with him anymore.

*Is it really that all of mankind has a very negative and harming attitude? Is it true that people from well-to-do backgrounds and from higher strata of society will not do anything as degrading as harm an innocent child? How can one take it for granted that relatives and loved ones will not harm you? Maybe my grandmother trusted my uncle a little more than he actually deserved to be trusted. Or maybe, I trusted my uncle a little more than I should have, whereas for him it was fulfilling his own needs and filling his own hunger that mattered more than the relationship between him and a girl who was fit enough to be his daughter isn't it? *

5th Incident - Fresh Peanuts

I was still young and innocent. I suppose, during the time of this incident I was in the 5th standard. The house that we used to live in at the time had a huge field in front it which was mainly used for farming. That farm land exists till date. Since that land was mostly used for farming, I came across a lot of people who were related to the agriculture sector. The quarters in front of our house was mostly inhabited by people from the agriculture sector who were transferred there. There was just one approach road in between the farm and our house and it ran right in front of our main gate. As a result, we would constantly come across people who lived in those quarters and over time used to become pretty well acquainted with them. In addition, most of the people who were transferred there were from upper Assam and they have an affinity towards becoming very friendly and can be extremely talkative. The field always bore a whole lot of fruits which we would normally pluck and the area was breathtakingly beautiful. Since it was a large area, every year we would also organize our annual picnics there.

There was once when two people were transferred there; one from Nowgaon and the other from Jorhat. To address them we would add "Uncle" to their last names. In a very short time, the "Uncle" from Nowgaon became very friendly with us. He was always full of life, very jovial and showed us a lot of affection. He was very good at math and would always help my brother who was preparing to get into a boarding school at the time. He always paid special attention to me and showed me a lot of affection. He would always get me some special treats whenever he visited and would also tutor me alongside my brother. I would visit him at his quarters and since he worked with the agriculture department, brought us various farm products like fresh peas, groundnuts, soya beans and the likes.

One day, as usual, he called me to his quarter to pick up some fresh groundnuts that had just arrived. I loved groundnuts and rushed almost immediately. I don't even remember if I had informed my mother. I still love groundnuts to this day; however, every time I eat them, I am taken back to that particular day. When I reached, the room looked like a warehouse full of huge packets filled with groundnuts. To this day, I still can't get the smell of the agricultural fertilizers that had engulfed the room out of my nose. He took a small plastic bag, filled it with peanuts and gave it to me. What I didn't notice is that, after I entered, he had silently closed and locked the door behind me.

Once I had had my fill of the groundnuts, he playfully took me to his bed. He lay on his back, picked me up on his stomach and started to tickle me. He said that we were playing a tickling game. But, that's not where it ended. In continuation of his acting playful, he suddenly turned me over and lay on top of me all the while tickling me. What I actually felt is that he was trying very hard to rub his pubic region against mine all the while groping my chest area very hard. I was young, but realized that what he was doing wasn't very decent. Also, my past experience helped me understand what was going on. I made up an excuse to try and get away from him as soon as the realization struck. He let me go, but with a warning not to tell anyone about the game, lest I people start to assassinate my character and call me foolish. I remember him also telling me that my mother would scold me and may be even spank me if I ever told anyone. Again I kept quiet just so that I wouldn't come out scathed.

I used to respect and adore that uncle. But, from that day on, whenever I came across the person, I would feel things that I find very hard to explain. All I know that they weren't at all feelings of cordiality; leave alone love or respect. The days went by and I did not breathe a word of the incident to anyone. But, things between us had changed. I stopped greeting him or talking to him the way

I did before. He was transferred out after some time, but my mother never questioned me about my sudden change in behavior towards him. Maybe she just didn't notice.

*It isn't that he was a young boy or was uneducated. Professionally he was from an officer's cadre. Despite that his behavior was absolutely unbecoming of someone of that class. There was a devilish attitude hidden behind that mask. I ask myself frequently. Why did he behave the way that he did? Was I to be blamed for being naughty? Is it possible that I incited him in any way because I would visit his quarters regularly? Or, is it that my parents believed in him blindly given his education background and social status? Perhaps he lacked any form of moral values! Or, could it be that the desire to satiate sexual hunger overrides everything else? *

6th Incident - Dharma

I used to believe in the rituals of prayers and worship from a very tender age. In fact, I would also observe almost every fast. I suppose it was the influence of being raised in a predominantly Bengali neighborhood. I recall hearing the sound of the conch right from the time I became more aware of my surroundings as a toddler. I would wake up to the sweet sounds of the prayers emanating from the nearby Satsang Vihar temple. And maybe that's why I still have a fondness towards Bengali cuisine. From Lakhi Puja to Holi to all other Hindu and Bengali festivities, our kitchen would be filled with Bengali dishes and sweets.

We were especially close to the Bengali family that lived behind our house. I don't really remember how and when we became that close, but all I remember is that the main lady of that house was like a mother to me. So much so that it won't be wrong of I claim that that lady actually raised me. The father, mother, 2 sons that were elder to me, and an older daughter. It was said that they had another son; the oldest who left home when he was a teenager not to ever return. As far as I know, that son still hasn't come home. The father had a business dealing in dried areca nuts and the mother; who I called Borma, was an ardent devotee of Goddess Kali. I was very close to Borma and we shared a very affectionate relationship. I learnt much of the Hindu culture and rituals from her. I also learnt to observe the fasting rituals from her and started observing fasts from when I was about 10 or 11 years old. They had married their daughter off at a very early age and even the older was already married by then. In fact, we were so close knit that when the younger son eloped with his wife, he hid her at our house first. We were so close that we were always there for each other during the good time and all the trying ones as well.

This happened before the younger son got married. Although we weren't related by blood, I considered him to be my actual brother. Raksha Bandhan, the festival where a sister ties a thread; a Rakhi, around her brother's wrist in exchange for a solemn oath of protection was never really part of the Assamese culture. It was only beginning to catch on at the time. Just because everyone else in our school celebrated the festival, we too would tie a "Rakhi" around the wrists of the 2 boys. It was a Raksha Bandhan day and as always I went to their house to tie the sacred thread around their wrists. Once all the rituals were done with, the younger one told me, "Accompany me to the terrace, I've got a gift waiting for you." I didn't find anything amiss at the time because he would occasionally bring me gifts and even give me some pocket money during the school recess: their shop was very close to my school. I was overjoyed at the anticipation of receiving a gift and followed him to the terrace without any questions asked. He fished out a 500 Rs note from his wallet and showed it to me. I still remember the amount because, to me, Rs.500.00 was a huge sum considering my age. As he handed the note to me he said, "I'll give you this note if you do something for me in return." I was elated and reached out to take the note from his hand. He handed me the note and then grabbed a chair that was lying there, sat in it and made me sit on his lap. He kept talking to me while he opened his jeans and then tried to rub his penis against my privates. I didn't understand. He showed that he loved me a lot and I had played on his lap many a time before, but on that day, the game seemed very unfamiliar; eerie even. I tried to get up and move away from him, but he held me tighter and asked me to stay a while longer. When I resisted, he said laughingly that he would take the note away from me. I stayed there a while longer, but when he made another attempt, he hurt me and I started to cry. He closed my mouth with his hand almost smothering me. I still very well remember that wicked smile on his face even today. Finding no way out, I bit his palm and he let go and I ran. Only that innocent, fragile little me could understand exactly how I felt then. I started detesting him from that day on and could only wish him harm. The best part is that all of this happened right on top of the area that housed their temple at home.

From then on I made it a point to only meet him when others were around. However, at every opportunity that he found me alone, he would flash his penis at me. And when this started to happen very frequently, I stopped going to their house altogether. The fact is that he continued such behavior even after he had gotten married.

He expired about 4 years ago because of a cancer that damaged his liver. He was last treated at a hospital in Guwahati where I live. My mother kept coaxing me to pay him a visit since he was in a serious state and was on his deathbed. As a good human being, I know I was supposed to at least pay him a visit, even if it was for that just one time. However, I just couldn't bring myself to do that.

I wish to know if it is possible to love someone unconditionally, maintain a relationship without any expectations or strings attached. Or, is it that relationships in actuality have no real value? Although Borma was very devout and knew most of the prayer rituals, did she conveniently neglect instilling basic moral values into her son? Is it possible that whatever happened to me was because of my attraction to gifts? Should I have not listened to him and followed him upstairs without having anyone else accompanying us? Or should I have been more judgmental about him? Is it my parents' fault for failing to teach me not to hanker after gifts and material benefits? Or was it simply because he didn't know how to control his sexual instincts? There are still many more questions that remain unanswered.

7th Incident- An educated teacher

An educated teacher, one of my father's cousins, who was elder to him, got married at an age that was quite beyond the normally socially acceptable age. In our culture, we consider even our father's cousin to be his brother and we would call him Bordeuta; meaning Uncle who is father's older brother. The marriage ceremonies took place at my grandmother's place in the village and was celebrated with a lot of pomp as almost everyone in the village were eagerly waiting for him to get married. As far as I can remember, I was in the 7th standard. I was overjoyed too. Not only did I get to be with almost all my cousins and most of all, the freedom and the affection that a child always gets at the grandmother's place.

Borma's (we call Bordeuta's wife Borma), maternal house was a little away from the town that we lived in and our house happened to be on the road connecting her house to our grandmother's. Borma had two younger brothers. The elder one was a teacher. Once when Borma was visiting her maternal home, she took me along. We planned to stay there for a while.

(For those unacquainted with the Assamese family culture, let me take this opportunity to explain how it works and how we address them. Just like cousins are considered to be brothers or sisters, even an uncle's wife is considered to be a mother figure in the Assamese culture. So, by default, even an uncle's wife's brother becomes our uncle and just like we address a mother's brother as mama, we begin to address even the aunt's brothers as mama.)

Now, Borma was absolutely new to our home and by default she got all the attention and affection. She in turn returned that love and affection to us kids. That night, considering that I was still very young, I was asked to go and sleep with the elder mama; the teacher. Maybe no one considered that anything could go wrong mainly because of the homely atmosphere that had built up between the two homes.

That night I came across another avatar of wickedness; in the form of a well educated teacher. I remember the night vividly. I was not only scared, but physically hurt and I cried the whole night through. I didn't know them very well; after all they were new acquaintances as my Borma and Bordeuta had just gotten married.

It was somewhere in the middle of the night. I woke up and found a hand on my chest. It wasn't anyone else's but the same mama's whose bed I was sleeping in. I was just about attaining puberty and my breasts were beginning to develop. He was slowly rubbing my nipples; I have no recollection if he tried to do anything else because I was deep in sleep till a while ago. All I remember is that my nipples were beginning to hurt because of the rubbing. Not only was I in an awful lot of pain, but I remember being scared to the bone. I turned to the side with my back to him and tried to wriggle as far away from him as I could. He let me go. But after a while, I could feel his hand on me again and he also bit my ear while whispering very softly, "Go to sleep quietly, everyone's fast asleep." I don't understand why I could do nothing at the time to protect myself and stayed like that the entire night bearing a tremendous amount of pain.

Even today, I am at a total loss of words to explain how I feel when I remember that night. I still feel sick when I think about it and all I can do whenever I feel that way is to slowly console myself that that was all in the past.

I got out of bed early in the morning before anyone else was awake and rushed to the washroom. My breasts were hurting and my nipples burning just like it does when you touch the ember of a dying fire. I kept splashing cold water on my nipples. When I checked properly, I noticed that they had been rubbed so hard that the black skin of the areola had peeled off and had turned red like there was a rash. I still shudder when I think of that day, but just like all the other times before, I couldn't bring myself to tell anyone about what had happened to me the night before.

Yes, after I got married, there was always an amount of conjugal harmony. I know, just like all normal men, even my husband finds that portion to be one of my body's best assets. However, there were many instances when I just would not allow him to even touch them. Then again, despite getting irritated and annoyed, there were times when I would just let go to maintain the harmony. I just couldn't understand why I'd get irritated whenever my husband, who I love dearly, tried to touch my breasts. I still remember the pain. In fact, even when my first child was born, I would hate to breastfeed him. Whenever he looked to feed off me, or when he'd pucker up to take the nipple in his mouth, that burning sensation would come rushing back. I still remember that my mother would silently place that innocent little child at my nipple whenever I was in deep sleep just so that I wouldn't know. Even then I couldn't muster the courage to tell anyone why I hated breastfeeding that poor little child who actually had no part to play except for giving in to his natural instinct of looking for his mother's milk.

*Who should I ask about that entire incident? Are people actually what they seem, or are they just wickedness behind some fancy masks? And that all pertinent questions right from the 1st incident; does love and kindness in a relationship have no value? Is it possible that even we take everything at face value and trust society and people blindly? Could it be that my Borma had not actually received the kind of education related to a man's behavior? Should my mother have just not allowed me to go to their place in the first instasnce and not trusted them so blindly? *

8th Incident - Bihu Function

This was the last time anything like this happened in the innocence of my youth. After this incident, I began to learn how to protect myself from being abused. I also began to understand more clearly which of my body parts were the main reason behind my being abused sexually, what was it that even my own and seemingly respectable people in society were looking for in me.

(This was just after my "Tuloni Biya". Again, let me take the privilege of informing those not very acquainted with Assamese culture what "Tuloni Biya" is all about. It's a ritual, almost like a wedding, that is conducted when a girl hits menstruation and gets her periods for the first time. It isn't a very pompous affair and is mostly attended by the elderly women of the family and close relatives.)

Well! Coming back to the point, this time, the perpetrator was no one else but one of our own direct relatives. The worst part is that no one will ever believe that he could harbor pedophilic instincts given his charismatic and friendly nature.

I had just cleared my 8th Standard exams and the "Tuloni Biya" rituals had just been done with. My mother, aunts, and cousins explained to me the nuances of the changes and that now I had to protect certain parts of my body, and what could happen if I got too close to men and all of that. All in all, that was when I received a semblance of a sex education. They all told me that I had to keep certain parts of my body covered at all times. Many people explained a lot of things to me little realizing that I had already endured the pain of all that they were talking about.

(Here I'm going take a short break for a bit and go back to relationships and the way we address them here in Assam. Remember how we address a father's elder brother; even a cousin as "Bordeuta"? Well! In a similar fashion we address the younger brother as "Dodaideu" and his wife as "Khuri". And since we are on the topic of the Assamese, let me also inform you that the major festivals of Assam, besides the religious ones, are Bhogali or Magh Bihu and Rongali/Bohag Bihu. Bhogali Bihu is celebrated mid January and the other in mid April of every year. Bhogali Bihu is a celebration of the harvest and there's a lot of feasting, whereas Rongali Bihu is the spring festival after which people start sowing for the next harvest. Rongali Bihu; which could become a month long celebration today, is normally celebrated with a lot of dance and music, some of which can go on all night.)

So, let's get back to the incident. One of my dad's cousins lived not very far from our house. He was younger to my dad and we would call him "Dodaideu". There would be a Rongali Bihu function held near his house every year and the organizing committee would always invite some of the Assamese celebrities to perform at the function. Rongali Bihu was just around the corner and that year's function they had called Zubeen Garg to perform. I was thrilled; I adored Zubeen Garg right from my childhood and loved his music. I wished to go see him perform in person, however there was no one who was willing to take me there.

It was Bihu day and as usual the house was filled with guests. My mother used to make an amazing Rohi; a traditional Ahom rice beer, and that was almost always what drew in all the guests. Dodaideu was also a part of the guests which made me very happy. That gave me an excuse to go back with Dodaideu and Khuri. The plan was to stay over just so that I could attend Zubeen Garg's program. Now, April is also the month when the pre-monsoons hit the region.

(There's a storm that the Assamese fondly call "Bordoisila" which appears in this month and it normally always coincides with the Bihu functions. When the storm hits, it is usually believed that Bordoisila was on her way to her mother's house. The storm is usually followed by a torrential downpour.)

Unfortunately, Bordoisila happened to pass through just on the day Zubeen was performing. Although the show went on, we couldn't make it to the venue and I sulkily settled to watch the program being telecast live on TV.

After the program, I went to bed with Dodaideu and Khuri. Khuri was the first one to get out of bed. I had woken, but feeling lazy from staying awake till late at night, I decided to laze around and lay in bed a while longer. Dodaideu was still lying beside me and seemed to be fast asleep. I was just dozing off when I felt a touch which made me feel uneasy and irritated. I could feel a hand on me and someone rubbing their pelvic region against my body. I was stunned for a moment mainly because I just couldn't fathom the thought of Dodaideu being that kind of a person. All my memories came rushing back and I came to my senses. I got up and stared angrily at Dodaideu. He immediately pretended to be fast asleep and behaved as though he didn't know what was going on. I got out of bed and rushed outside. Khuri was sitting there and I looked at her. I saw her looking at me lovingly and if I did want to say anything, I just clammed up. Or maybe it was just that I was maturing enough to think better than to say anything that might hurt her.

Dodaideu woke up sauntered out of the room late. He saw me but couldn't look me in the eyes. I had decided by then that I would go home and tell my mother everything that had happened. Everything changed by the time I reached home though. I just bottled it all up, didn't say a word and hurt myself once again.

*Who was he really? Was he just another pervert in the disguise of a decent human being, or was he just another criminal? I sometimes also ask myself if it was actually good that he behaved that way because it helped me remember what I had to go through in the past! Or is it just that he did not have a very satisfying sex life with Khuri? Perhaps he just didn't cherish or value relationships including the one he shared with Khuri! Or was he just a bookworm who learnt everything by rote and didn't know how to apply them to his life and was devoid of any moral values? *

More reasons and situations

It's a myth that old men aren't sexually active. Believing that myth and trusting an old man, we mostly feel absolutely safe to leave our children with him unattended. The truth is that many times, children fall victims to the lust of old men too. It's been scientifically proven that many males remain sexually virile till about 85 years of age. Unfortunately most elderly men remain sexually starved since most of their wives become frigid by then owing to hormonal changes, gynecological issues, daily life problems and the likes. In most cases of the elderly indulging in child abuse, it is found that they had lost absolute control of their sense owing to their unfulfilled sexual urges and decide to prey on the weakest link, the ones that trust them and can't fight back; children. That is why it is of utmost importance to ensure that the child doesn't have t suffer due to the parents' negligence.

Not just ours; the Ahom society, but even in many other cultures, alcohol flows like water and it is customary to have a drink, especially around occasions. I'm not saying that the consumption of alcohol is a sin or should be banned. But it's always good to be aware of people who can't stomach alcohol, lose self control and don't have any idea about what they're doing or saying. We read or watch such cases in the news almost every other day, and also know of quite a few people who lose absolute control once they've had a little to drink. In that case, how is it possible to entrust the child to the care of a person who can't handle herself or himself once drunk?

Important and unacceptable behavior

It was 2013, just one year after my 2nd child was born and I had just completed my 24th birthday. That's when I realized the deeper ramifications of what had happened to me. I still remember that day very vividly. I yelled, I cried, I sobbed, and all those bottled up emotions, feelings came rushing out and I felt a sense of relief. That's the same day I narrated everything to my husband before telling my mother. Actually, something happened that night; which will be revealed later, that triggered it all and made that dam that I had built all the while burst.

That's when I got rid of all the shame, guilt, anger and resentments and could face my perpetrator and look them in the eyes without and fear or self doubt.

The surprising thing is that when I narrated the incidents to my mother, instead of showing any form of sympathy or empathy, she charged at me cynically saying, "You've certainly done something great. You've defamed your own mama in the eyes of your husband, and you expect your husband to accept you just as you are now." I suppose that's the very response that I had been expecting all my life and that's why I neglected telling on my perpetrators and buried my feelings deep in my heart till I could bear it no longer.

Why did my mother react the way she did? Was it because she feared what society would think of me, or was she just scared that my husband would now begin to taunt me and eventually even desert me? Or was it just that she loved my brother more than she loved either one of us sisters? There's a definite 19 possibility though, that just like how many others deal with shocking news even she was just unable to accept the reality.

I was raised in a very strict environment. Just like many others' in this country, even my parents' views on sex and exposure to any sexual content was very orthodox. Leave alone sex scenes, even if the movie showed some kind of kissing scenes or any form of love making, the TV would be switched off or we would be sent to fetch something from another room. And if we didn't budge or allow the TV to be switched off, we would be reprimanded.

In actuality, it would be better if a sense of openness is maintained between parents and children. Parents could take some time to explain what the scene was all about and what it meant in context to the movie. At the same time, in case the child is a toddler, the parent could ask them jokingly if anyone has touched them like that. They could also be told that no one else is allowed to touch them like that without permission except for the parents; and depending on the situation, only the mother. And once they reach adulthood that it should be restricted to either the partner or their spouse. That is when children stop being confused and learn to differentiate between a good touch and a bad one. It's always essential that they start learning this at an early age and also to discuss if they've seen anything like this happening to any of their friends or other children that they come across. Instead of being a strict parent and manipulating the child using anger or superiority, it's always advisable to maintain a friendly and approachable nature. This could also help the parents save the child even before the situation gets out of hand and the child lands into even deeper trouble. Can there be a more fulfilling and better relationship than a child finding their best friends in their parents?

Like all other parents, even my parents taught me to always tell the truth and never lie. However, whenever I confessed to being naughty or not being able to perform academically, I would not only get scolded, but also beaten at times. The fact is I got to know only a month before I started writing this book that I'm dyslexic and have a learning disorder. But no one realized what my problem was and why my academic performance was not really at par. Although both my parents were very strict, my mother was stricter and would mete out the punishments. I'd always be frightened because I would never know when and why my mother would get angry and blast out. Maybe it was because of this strictness that I could never confide in my mother and bottled everything up till I was 23 years old although she took a lot of pains to raise me and my siblings.

Like I mentioned earlier, I don't entirely blame my parents. They did their best with whatever they had learnt as they were growing, and most of their learning was old fashioned and orthodox, things that had been passed along through generations. Perhaps, finding no other way out, in the midst of all other pressures, they believed that the only way to rectify a child was by punishing them, either physically or mentally. And maybe that's applicable to many other households, not only then, but even till date.

However, this can break a child's spirit; at times even lead to depressive behavior. Besides, there may be many other cases or situations where we carelessly refuse to see things from the child's perspective and try and use our own methods to control and manipulate the child to conform to our norms.

And continuously failing to understand and empathize with the child can lead to them becoming overtly depressed and mentally disturbed, developing a criminal mindset, becoming aimless and without any ambition, and suicidal tendencies. Isn't it equally important to allow a child to grow with a positive attitude, facilitate a guided learning process and not just condition their minds to conform to our standards? I would like to request you to think about this deeply.

The poor, the destitute, and the orphans

There are many children who live on the streets, in orphanages, or even with their parents; some privileged and some not very, who have become victims of sex abuse at some point or the other. And yet, we consider our society to be a developed and civilized one. In every street, every corner, police stations, or even if you ask around the neighborhood that you're in, you'll come across cases of child abuse that'll give you goose bumps and make your hair stand on end. There are many boys and girls who've either taken begging or a life of crime or have begun prostituting themselves; some for the basic essentials, some because they've gotten addicted to chemicals or alcohol, where as some just so that they can afford a better way of life. There are many such children, who finding no way out, fall prey to sex predators and pedophiles.

Most people from a so called decent society look down upon prostitutes and ostracize them. But, would you like to really know why they become one? Why do they start to rent their bodies out? Many children who have suffered sexual abuse begin to develop a sense of curiosity. Also, due to lack of proper sex education, they fail to understand the value of their sexual organs. In addition, when they are abused continuously from their childhood, they transgress the thin line between pain and pleasure and it becomes more of a habit. And these people in turn start abusing even more children and the chain just keeps going on and on; just because the kids weren't properly educated on moral principles and sexual ethics.

Through my own experiences that I've shared in this memoir, I wish to make an appeal to the education departments not only in this state but also across the the country. The appeal is a very simple. I sincerely hope that sex education becomes an integral part along with the regular academic syllabus mainly so that children do not remain misinformed and also learn how to protect themselves from sex abuse from an early stage. The aim is to try and bring down cases of child abuse; sexual or mental, and so that we as parents feel absolutely safe when our children leave home every day; either for school, or to socialize. And since it's the children or the youth that hold the key to the future, once they are protected, they will lead the way for the future generations to a world much more righteous and ethical. There are generally humungous funds allocated to industries, city or town planning and the likes. Even if a fraction of that amount is added to the education departments to facilitate the addition of sex education, I think it'll go a long way in helping curb the sexual abuse of minors and children.

And this shouldn't only be limited to public or private schools, but should also be extended to teaching kids who live on the streets, are poor, unsheltered and destitute. That way, even the crime graphs may come down to a great extent. If every profit making or not-for-profit organization also join hands to reach out to the child in the street, the slums or in orphanages, many of these kids might actually be saved from the horrors of sexual abuse and see a brighter future and look forward to living a decent life becoming productive and responsible citizens of the country. If the government makes teaching this mandatory, kids will learn how to protect themselves and what they need to do in case they've fallen victim, in which case I reckon that the number of sex related crimes will also drop drastically.

Most people associate respectability and status only with education and job profile, the more the certificates, the higher the hierarchy, the more the respect. As a result, most parents primarily focus only on the child's educational qualifications and the career path. Tell me, how many parents actually think that instilling ethical values and proper sex education also play very important roles in the holistic development of a child? How many parents can safely say, without any doubt in their minds that their children have never been abused sexually even if it is to a mild extent? Maybe no one has actually given it a second thought and has taken things for granted thinking that this can never happen to us or our children.

The after effects of abuse

The moment parents get to know about something is wrong and that their child may have fallen prey to sex abuse, some file police complaints, whereas a majority avoid complaining and try and hide it just so that they can try and live normal life in their society. However, there are some parents who never find out. Imagine what those children must be going through; a silent torture that penetrates into their very soul of existence every day and every moment.

I speak from my own experience. After all that happened and I got into the habit of not telling anyone and bottling everything up, I started detesting myself, hating the organs that make me a woman, In fact, I was so disturbed that I actually tried to end it all in 2006.

I wouldn't feel safe even in my own home. That was because, out of ignorance of my plight, my parents still maintained good relationships with my abusers. I would always want to shout and tell my parents, "Please don't maintain any more relationships with them. They hurt your daughter and are not very good people", but I would be scared. I could never see the good side of sex and sexual relationships, I wouldn't even try. At times I would touch my woman parts. I resented the perpetrators and would get livid with anger every time I saw them. In fact, I would want to actually kill them at the first opportune moment. That's how aggressive I had become. I could do nothing else other than abusing and cursing them. On e died and some of the others now have daughters of their own. I want to ask them if they've tried to do the same things to their daughters as they did with me and how they would feel as a father if their daughters were also sexually abused and exploited.

But now that I've realized and understood that all these have happened in the past and I need to let go, I am learning how to deal with my feelings. I used to detest all males, wouldn't want to trust them in any way, always doubted their intentions if they ever touched me even generally. I would get into many unnecessary arguments if a man ever touched me, even if it was by mistake. That's exactly how almost all victims of child sex abuse grow up. In case the parent ever files a police complaint, imagine how the victim goes through the trauma and relives the incident when they are cross questioned during interrogation. Also try and imagine how helpless that a child feels when the parents try and hide the fact that they were abused sexually and ask them to keep quiet and not tell anyone because the parents are more bothered about what society will think of them.

Think about the child who can't tell anyone that she/he has become a victim of sex abuse. Try and visualize how lonely and frightened that poor, innocent little soul must be feeling thinking about what happened and why. Even it is just the one time, the child doesn't get abused just once; they are reminded by the police, the judiciary and above all the society. But one thing is for sure, the little soul definitely lives and relives that horrific incident their entire lives in their heads. All these only a victim can understand well.

After Marriage

Chapter 2
Page 1

The first meeting:

October 2004

It was Dussehra day, the last day of Durga Puja. My brother and my mother had gone to my grandmother's and I was at my Borma's place behind our house. My little sister came running saying "Papa's calling you home, Chetia Khura is here". Chetia Khura wasn't exactly a relative; neither close nor extended. However, he was just like family, considered him as a parent to me and felt absolutely safe around him. He was the son of one of my father's teachers in his school days. All of us adored Chetia Khura tremendously.

Even before my sister could finish speaking, I dashed home to the living room where he was sitting and went straight for the seat right next to him as was my habit. In fact, everyone would tell me that this was a habit from when I was very young. In fact, if I knew that he was at home with us, he was the first person I looked for when I woke in the morning. I had actually gone to the extent of calling him Maa. That's how much I loved and trusted him. But that day was different. There was already someone else; a young man, sitting besides him; someone I didn't know. Chetia Khura introduced the guest as the son of his maternal uncle; his cousin, who lived in Guwahati and had come to visit. Chetia Khura brought him along since the young man was feeling bored. I got introduced, greeted the new guest and went into the kitchen to get some tea and snacks to serve to the guests. We chatted for a while and when it was time to leave, the young guest kept turning around to look at me and kept waving goodbye. I though it kind of odd, but he was a guest after all.

A week later, when I came home from my tuitions, I found Chetia Khura sitting in the living room. In my unbridled joy at seeing him, I rushed and sat directly in his lap. He turned my face around, looked me in the eyes and said, "You've become a very big girl now little one." All I could say was "Have you noticed only now? I became a big girl a long time ago." The fact is that I had just completed my 10th standard pre-board exams and was preparing to appear for the board exams.

Dad's leaves were over and he was preparing to re-join duty. He was hurrying through his meal and mom asked me to go inside and put my bag away. As I was walking away I overheard my dad telling Chetia Khura, "She's still too young, I haven't really thought about anything yet." I reached my room to find Maina; that's what we called my little sister, sitting there quietly. The moment she saw me, she could not control herself anymore and blurted out, "Remember that young man who had come with Chetia Khura the other day? Well! It seems he wants to marry you." I was shocked and at a complete loss for words. I desperately wanted to find out what was going on. Chetia Khura left and my mother walked into the room and the first thing she asked me was, "What were you wearing that day?" "A skirt and a top", is what I said and she left without asking me anything else.

It was decided that Chetia Khura would have lunch at our place and his maternal uncle and his cousin would accompany him too. The primary objective was for my mother to get to know the uncle and his family since she had missed out on meeting them the other day. Although quite a few things had already been discussed over the phone, this meeting was more of a "Getting to know each other better" kind. It was mainly decided that I would be married off to Chetia Khura's cousin; the same one that came visiting, once I had completed my graduation.

Chetia Khura's uncle and family coming over for lunch was like a grand event. After all, this was the first major wedding proposal that I had received. It's not that I hadn't received wedding proposals before. However, I was younger then. It's a possibility that my built had confused many people. Also, I was always told that I was attractive enough for people to actually notice. Well! We were all introduced properly this time and we all got talking. I couldn't speak much because I had a million butterflies in my stomach and kept visiting the washroom just to try and escape. I was in a complete state of confusion. Finally the young man and I were left alone to talk. The first thing he said is, "I definitely like you a lot, what do you have to say about it?" "My parents know best and I will do whatever they say," is all I could come up with. He gave me his phone number and asked me to stay in touch so that we could get to know each other even better. My mother knew that he had given me his number.

I was young and didn't understand what was going on. One day, I mentioned it jokingly to my friends at school that I had received a marriage proposal and also gave them the details. One day my friends dared me to call him and said that if he really loved you, he will come right away. After all he was a person from Guwahati, the big city, and such men are not to be trusted. Going with the flow of the joking dare, I actually did call him and ask him to visit right away.

A few days later I received a phone call from him saying that he was in my town and had come specifically to see me. I went to Chetia Khura's house to visit him. With everyone's permission, we went out on a drive; just the two of us. At first I was absolutely fine, but a sudden fear overcame me. I became absolutely silent and crouched as much as I could; sticking to my side of the door. He took one look at me and started to tease and laugh at me continuously all through the drive.

Chapter 2
Page 2

December 7th, 2004

Honking loudly, a car stopped at our gate suddenly that evening. We ran outside to see Chetiya Khura in the car along with the person I was supposed to get married to. We came to know only later that it was my fiancé's birthday and he had arrived from Guwahati to celebrate with us. (I use the term fiancé here for the sake of convenience although we hadn't been engaged formally till then). Our house was bustling with activity again like it was another big event. The actual purpose though was for his family to try and convince my dad to get me married off at the earliest and not to delay it. After a lot of discussions and convincing my father finally agreed to get me married off after I had appeared for my 12th exams. Everyone was happy even though my dad did expect that he'd get some more time. Mainly, somewhere deep inside, I suppose even I was happy.

The birthday celebrations were held at Chetia Khura's house the next day. While I was talking to my fiancé, he suddenly hugged me and tried to caress me lovingly. After all, I was his fiancé, wasn't that's the least he would expected; a return hug or for him to be acknowledged kindly. Instead, I felt disgusted and I ran into the washroom and had a bath rubbing myself vigorously like I had just been smeared with something really dirty and disgusting.

When I got back from the bath, he looked at me sadly and in a very dejected tone asked me, "What happened? Why did you rush to have a bath? Do I disgust you so much?" I honestly didn't have any answer to his questions. I was just as confused myself. I really didn't know why I moved away from him that way.

Dinner was planned at our place that very evening and my fiancé was supposed to stay over that night. While dinner preparations were on, I got busy packing for a music video shoot scheduled for the next day. Just in case I haven't mentioned it before, I was a professional Bihu dancer and had featured in a few music videos that year. I was actually in the midst of shooting for that particular music album when my marriage was finalized; something that my fiancé strongly disapproved of. He was angry when he saw me packing and getting ready for the next day and also got into a slight disagreement with my father over it. He couldn't fathom the thought of me going for a shoot with others when he had already accepted me as his wife. My father tried his best to explain to him that everything had already been scheduled before the marriage proposal and that backing out at this stage would mean burning bridges with the people involved in production house.

Early next morning my fiancé left the house in a huff although he was supposed to leave only after lunch. Along with myself, we were all very surprised; however, I got busy packing up to leave for the shoot. A few hours later Chetia Khura arrived at our house saying that my fiancé had reached Chetia Khura's place. He said that my fiancé was literally sobbing that despite expressing his absolute displeasure, I was adamant and wanted to go ahead and shoot a video with absolute strangers. Everyone was disturbed and it was finally decided that my video shooting schedules would be cancelled and everyone proceeded to Chetia Khura's house to try and pacify my fiancé.

While pacifying my fiancé, it was suddenly decided by the afternoon that the ring ceremony to formalize the wedding would take place immediately. The excuse was that I was still very young and in the fickle mindset normally associated with young people, I might fall in love with someone else and eventually end up breaking the marriage plans. And since he loved me a lot and wanted only me as his wife, his family and he thought it best to initiate the formalities as per our customs and traditions; mainly so that my mind wouldn't wander. Everyone got busy making the arrangements. My mother came home for a while and I could see that she was in tears since I was getting formally engaged; and that too without much warning.

But, shouldn't someone have asked me what I wanted? Did I want to continue the shooting program and perhaps even take it up as a career option, or did I want to wear a ring and get engaged? Was my permission necessary too? Or didn't my likes, wants and needs had any value? Why did my parents not give me the privilege to exercise my rights or freedom of choice? Why is it that this society still thinks it unnecessary to consult the girl before getting her married of? Were the wants of a stranger weighed heavier than mine?

By nightfall, my fiancé's family arrived along with his elder sister. They were all very happy and I finally wore his ring amidst a whole lot of merriment; especially on the boy's side of the family. It was also decided then that I would get married the moment I had completed my 10th standard exams. As I was very young and everyone unanimously decided that I would be treated as their daughter and they would also allow completing my graduation. There were many deals struck and many agreements made. It was like I was in some kind of a conference room or a darbar. Instead of discussing all that, perhaps they should have asked me what I wanted. To this date I'm still trying to figure out what exactly was I feeling that day.

The next day he came home. All of my friends were there too. They were shocked that the ring ceremony took place so suddenly and had come to enquire. After dinner, as everyone was getting ready to go to bed, he suggested that he help all of us with our studies. We agreed considering that the final exams weren't too far away. We enjoyed the study session and there was a lot of laughter. Finally my friends went off to bed leaving just the two of us alone. We started speaking, and he was talking about himself and his life. After all we didn't really find time to get to know each other. He started to tell me how much he loved me and what all he had had planned after we were married. He explained how he would take care of me and how he would always shower me with his love and affection. I was confused too to hold myself back when he tried to be intimate and so went with the flow. I was petrified and somehow I didn't really like what was happening. I wanted to refuse but I just couldn't bring myself around to say no. Eventually I just let myself go and we got physically intimate.

He left the next afternoon promising to take care of me always and how he would love me always. A couple of days later I tried to narrate what happened that night. However, I still don't know if my mother just feigned not to understand what I was saying or, was I just not able to explain everything clearly, because my mother just didn't react.

On the 28th of December 2004, my mother and Chetiya Khura went to Guwahati to visit my fiancé's home in Guwahati. After all, everything happened so suddenly that no one actually had the time to complete the actual responsibility of verifying the credentials of my to-be in-laws. This was also partially because my parents trusted Chetiya Khura completely and relied on his judgment knowing that he would never knowingly let us down. And once again, the date of my marriage was brought forward to the 17th of January 2005; even before my 10th standard exams were to begin.

All the arrangements for the wedding were made. I only went with the flow; listening to everyone's advice, learning whatever I could about wedlock, and trying my best to do the things I was told to do to prepare myself for a happily married life. I felt like I was some kind of a machine or a robot that was being programmed to follow certain commands and act accordingly. In just about 15 days I was made to learn the kind of etiquette that must be displayed at all times; how to behave with my in-laws and my husband. In fact, I was also given a crash course on basic cooking techniques. It was like I was being readied for a soon to erupt war.

Chapter 2
Page 3

17th Jan 2005 – The Big Day

It was the big day, a day that most brides-to-be eagerly wait for. I, however, in that confused state of a teen's mind, didn't really know what was going on, leave alone understand what I was supposed to even feel. My friends had come over and in the naivety of our youth, we were dancing, joking and laughing knowing little of what awaited me. Only when the groom and his brigade arrived and I was surrounded by the ladies of the family; singing wedding songs and dressing me up, did I realize what was going on and I started to cry and pleaded to my mother not to get me married. But all my heart rendering sobs were lost in that din of wedding songs, chants and music and pleas were left unanswered. And when all the wedding rituals were done with and I was saying my goodbyes to my parents and the rest of my family, my father just told me three things that I still remember and try my best to live up to even today.

What he said is

1. Patience is the only key to success

2. Bring home a bag of areca nuts, but never a bag of gossip. (Greeting someone with betel leaf and areca nut is a custom in Assam and it's also a means of showing respect and hospitality)

3. Be like water, fluid and taking on the shape of the vessel that it's in.

I bent down and touched all the elders' feet as is the customary way to show respect and seek everyone's blessings. However, when it was time for me to leave, I clung on to my father refusing to leave. I wailed and I cried, but to no avail. Some tried to explain to me that everything was done and there's no way out; some resorted to murmuring cynically; and my mother, while half-dragging and half-carrying me to the car that was waiting to take me away said, "What is it that you want? Do you want to disgrace the family honor?" Many in the crowd only assumed that I was just sad like all other brides at the thought of leaving home. They tried to console me and convince me not to cry and to leave happily. Only I knew what I felt. I was terrified at the very thought of having to leave home and live the rest of my life with a total stranger.

Everything happened so fast that I was, in a manner of speaking, almost breathless. I lost track of time and I didn't even know when I transgressed from being a giggly teenager to assuming the roles and responsibilities of a homemaker. The irony of it all was that everyone thought me to be too young to ask me about my decisions or points of view on any matter, however, they didn't think me too young to get me married. In fact, I was not even of marriageable age as per the laws of the land.

I am still genuinely surprised by the double standards adopted by most elders. I was always taught to respect the decisions of elders and abide by their decisions without questioning. They are the ones who know best since they have the requisite experience and will never do anything that is detrimental. However, my question to everyone is, "Are you above the law?" "Why do many of you still get girls married off even before they come of an age of understanding?" "Why do you go against the laws and why don't you try and understand that teenage girls aren't capable of taking on the responsibilities of a homemaker?" Teenage girls are who they are; still in a phase of learning and unable to completely cope with the responsibilities of marriage.

No one has the right to marry a girl off at such a tender age. In fact, no one also has the right to enforce marriage on a girl even after she turns `18; the legal age for marriage. I would like to know how many families enforce marriage on a boy when he turns 18. Almost all families wait for the boy to complete his education, embark on a career path, become self-dependent and attain some amount of financial, social and mental stability before getting him married. Why don't the same rules apply to girls? I understand the many excuses that most families have; financial issues, the girl might fall in love and elope, the proposing boy and his family are well settled, and the likes. Why is it that the same rules don't apply to the girl's side of the family? Most families take the girl child to be a burden and wait for an opportune moment to get her married. And it's this thought process that has been the cause for many girls either being killed or abandoned across history; a practice that is still prevalent in many places across the country even today despite many stringent laws have been enacted. Perhaps, and I say this with a lot of cynicism, the practice of killing the girl child should've been allowed to continue. Perhaps that way, many girls wouldn't have to bear the kind of torture and harassment of being taken for granted, having no say in her life, and being married off at an early age against her wishes. At least she won't have her life wasted away after a few years of being happy.

In many cases, a girl's life is somewhat akin to that of a sacrificial lamb; fed, loved, made to feel at ease and then suddenly, instead of chopping off the head, she's married off; and no one cares to ask what she wishes. Does she want to study; does she want to embark on a career path, and does she want to be self-dependent? Nada, nothing; almost everyone doesn't seem to care. The match is a good one, the boy is well settled and his family is very good, let's just get her married. No one seems to care if she's ready or if she has made up her mind to get married. Even today, many families start saving; not for her education or for her to find her own path, but for her marriage. Right from a very young age, she is nurtured for life of wedlock; starting from home chores to cooking to adopting certain behavior patterns; just so that she can adapt herself from the moment she is married. However, if many families start to allow the girl to grow up to be educated and more self-reliant, she'll automatically have more self esteem and will be a much stronger person. And that way, crimes against women like rape, and physical and mental torture, cases of depression and suicide will automatically take a downward turn. Then again, whose responsibility is this, the governments or society at large? Is she some kind of a property that can be exchanged or is she supposed to be the pride of a family? I suppose everyone has the answers to these questions. It's just that no one wants to admit that they do, and even if they do admit, they don't want the answers and solutions to be implemented.

Chapter 2
Page 4

I travelled about 500 Kilometers, crying or sobbing almost all of the way. Taking solace only in the promises that my husband made to me and whole lot of consolation and convincing by the relatives and friends that came along to "deliver" me, I set foot into my husband's house in Guwahati. My new family welcomed me into their home with a whole lot of love, affection and respect. I was absolutely tired, but there were a few rituals that needed to be completed after which I was allowed to rest for a bit. The next day, after completing all the other rituals that had to be finished, all the people that accompanied me left. Chetiya Khura stayed back a while and left only later that night without informing me because I would have thrown a tantrum otherwise. When I think back to that day when I was left all alone in a house full of strangers, I still have tears in my eyes. I felt absolutely helpless, lonely even amongst a whole lot of people. I still find it very difficult to explain what I was feeling. I suppose what I felt as a teenager could not be comprehended by others.

That night I was told to share the bed with my husband. It was supposed to be a very special night. No one tutored me about what I was supposed to do. All I remembered then was what a cousin of mine had told me after she had gotten married and what Chetiya Khuri told me. On this special night I was supposed to do exactly as my husband wanted, and was not supposed to refuse anything. I was to do everything possible to keep my husband happy and satisfied.

And that's exactly what I did that night. My husband made love to me several times that night. I was tired and sleepy, but I didn't refuse him at all, despite the fact that was having a hard time bearing it. I wasn't at all aroused sexually. I also suppose that it was because I just wasn't of age and mental bearing as yet up till then. There was just this one thing that I knew because I had been hearing it since childhood; "Patti Parmeshwar", meaning the husband is like God.

And thus began my life of marriage. I could never refuse any of his sexual advances and did exactly as he wanted. Perhaps I had lost the habit of refusal somewhere during my childhood. I suppose that's why he could never figure out that I wasn't really enjoying it at all and in fact I wasn't very happy with him. Leave alone the mental agony; I couldn't refuse him even when my whole body was aching. Not to say that my husband wasn't loving or caring. He showered me with all love and affection that he could and would bring me whatever I wanted and would try his level best to keep me happy and contented at all times.

The days went by and I slowly started to get the feeling that I had unwittingly walked into a trap of child abuse. Even if I wanted to, I couldn't bring myself to running away, or hiding, or even telling someone about how I felt. After all, I was tutored that whatever happens between a husband and wife in the bedroom should remain in the bedroom itself. But I really didn't know why.

I only started thinking about all these things after it was very late into the marriage. Shouldn't he have sought my permission first? Shouldn't he have asked me if I was ready to be physically intimate? Am I satisfied with the experience or am I unhappy? I would drop subtle hints about my displeasure, wanting him to quickly satisfy himself and leave me alone. But I reckon that he never understood those hints because he never asked if I really was interested or not. Perhaps it was also due to my age that I didn't really know what sexual satisfaction was about and what it was supposed to feel like. It's a guess that there were times when he would feel that I wasn't actually very cooperative or that I didn't enjoy it much because there were times when he would bring me medicines to enhance my sexual urges, which I would consume without any questions. In fact, to prove that I am a good wife to him and just that I appear just as willing to have sex as my husband did, I would watch X-rated movies with him, try and do the things that the actors did.

I had begun to believe that the medicines and the movies would work and perhaps even I would begin to develop sexual urges. However, nothing seemed to work; maybe because I still hadn't actually come of age and the sexual instincts hadn't developed.

A few days after my wedding, I began to bleed. It wasn't time for my cycle to kick in as yet. I was taken to their family doctor who looked me up and laughingly said that these were the after effects of marriage. Now when I look back, I think that's when I had actually lost my virginity. What really is the purpose of a marriage? Is it sex? I still fail to understand. If the sole reason behind a marriage is sex, then I am against the whole system of marriage. After all, it's common knowledge that even unmarried couples too enjoy sex; especially in today's day and time.

Chapter 2
Page 5

A little while after marriage I went home to appear for my 10th standard school board exams. On coming back, I got to spend more time with my in-laws. That's when I got to know that they were originally from a village and that they were very orthodox even when it came to the dress code. As a result I was not to wear any kind of western or non-Assamese attire, but had to don the traditional Assamese Mekhela-Sador at all times. Again, for the benefit of readers not acquainted with Assamese attire, the Mekhela-Sador is a kind of lehenga and a cloth draped around the body somewhat in the form of a saree. It is made of cotton or silk, the silk ones usually reserved for special occasions. Now I was not accustomed to wearing a mekhela-sador at all times and was mostly very uncomfortable. I am sure that most women who have had to wear a saree for the first time will empathize with how uncomfortable I felt. I would always remain patient and wait for my husband to obtain permission to allow me to also wear dresses that I felt comfortable in. However, he just couldn't bring himself around to getting that permission from his parents. Although I was still new to the city, it was pretty difficult for me to abide by all the rules that normally apply to the rural areas. I was supposed to be the first one to be up every morning, start with the home chores, and even cook; things that I wasn't completely accustomed to and despite all of that I had to abide by an entire set of rules and regulations; rules that I knew existed, but never had to follow. There were a lot of changes that I had to adapt to.

I tried my best to adapt to the rules and follow them to the tee; unquestioning and unwavering. I suppose, till date, no one can point to me and say that I ever refused to do what I was told to do and how I was told to do it. I never argued back or said a word out of place even when anyone spoke with me in a rough tone; knowingly or unknowingly. I was hurt; emotionally and physically, yet I tried to give my best. I would, at times cry or throw tantrums in front of my husband, but I had no choice. There was no one I could talk to, no one I could share what I was going through with.

It was decided before the marriage that my in-laws wouldn't impose too many restrictions on my dress code. They had also agreed not to rely on me completely to do the household chores as; keeping my age in mind; I hadn't been shown the ropes adequately. Besides, the marriage happened so unexpectedly and quickly that no one had enough time to take me through the nuances of being a homemaker. In fact, even my husband had promised; not just to my parents, but also to me, that no one would impose any form of restrictions on me and that my studies would not be hampered at all. Despite all the promises, my world turned topsy-turvy and everything went haywire. I was lost and my dream bubble burst. I felt like I was slowly losing my grip on who I was and who I am.

I had almost no knowledge about being intimate and how to protect myself from becoming pregnant. No one explained all that to me. Besides, even though my husband was older and academically more qualified than I was; he was studying for his law degree at the time; even he lacked the basic information related to contraception. Considering that we have an age gap of about 16 years and he was 33 at the time when I was just 16, he should have been better informed. And that's how, at the age of 16 and just 3 months into my marriage, I found myself pregnant. Although everyone else was happy from deep within, I was scared and helpless. I had no clue about how to live and enjoy a married life, leave alone becoming a mother to a child. To this day, I still regret the fact that I couldn't enjoy my first pregnancy the way most other women usually do, especially when they're expecting the first child.

Chapter 2
Page 6

The days passed by. Although I was mentally not at ease, I tried my best to fit into every role that I had to assume. Playing the role of a dutiful wife; giving all the moral support that he needed and also satisfying his physical urges, that of the respectful and obedient daughter-in-law, and also of a sister-inlaw to both of my husband's brothers. Although my brothers-in-law were elder than I was, by agreement of the relationship status accorded by society, I automatically became their elder. Thus I also had to maintain that air of authority, responsibility, and maturity despite my age. I had to act and behave like a grown up at all times. This took its own toll and I was mostly never at ease. I suppose this is what can be constituted to be a form of mental torture. And through it all, I also had another life growing inside of me; a life that I had no clue how to take care of. I would only follow everyone's advice without even thinking about the consequences since I didn't know any better.

My board exam results were declared in the month of June. I didn't score very well; however, I still nurtured the thought of going to college. After all, my husband did promise that he wouldn't cause any hindrance in my studies. Unfortunately, a huge argument started off between my in-laws and my parents. My in-laws vehemently opposed my going to college mainly because, first and foremost, I was their daughter-in-law and second because I was pregnant. In fact one of my brothers-in-law put it in my husband's head saying, "She'll go to college, meet new friends; some of them will be boys, and she might just change her mind". He also mentioned that he had heard instances of a girl breaking up a marriage once she had become adequately educated. Considering that he was about 14 years older than I was, I kept that respect and didn't say a word; even though he had, in a manner of speaking, assassinated my character. A variety of arguments ensued about why I shouldn't go to college.

Despite all the arguments and much against my in-laws wishes, my husband, true to his word and some pressure from my parents, finally got me admitted to a college. I was 5 months into my pregnancy then but had not stopped dreaming. I dreamt about completing my 12th, about my first day at college, making new friends in the city. I was truly happy. More than anything else, what made me even happier was that I would be allowed to wear Kurtas and Pyjamas, since that was a part of the college uniform. If anyone asks about my experience about my first day at college, I describe it, however, there's always a hint of sadness in my tone. That's because, on the very first day, I got ready, donned my new

KurtaPyjama and when I went to say goodbye to my mother-in-law she looked at me dejectedly and said, "I'll cook the meal for everyone in the house, but when you get back you cook your own food". Only I know what I felt like. All that excitement and happiness about the first day at college just went up in smoke.

After all, the first day of college is normally a special day for all youngsters. In fact, even when I went to call on my father-in-law, she blocked my path and said, "He's sleeping. And it's best if you don't show yourself to him this way since you're dressed in a Kurta-Pyjama". I respected her decision and came away without saying a bye to my father-in-law. However, when I went to sit in the car, I noticed my husband's sister's son. He was slightly older than I was and it was his first day at college too. I knew that because he and I had both appeared for the board exams just that year. I noticed that my mother-in-law was extra loving towards him, kissing him and wishing him well on his first day. I saw all of that and once in the car, I couldn't help but cry and think of home.

This was supposed to be my society, my home, but why didn't I feel like I belonged here? In actuality, we've complicated simple relationships with a whole lot of rules and regulations. I need to know why a daughter-in-law can't be treated at par with one's daughter. Why is the newly wedded bride made to feel like she's the lone player in a football match against the entire husband's household? Who's responsible for that? Why is she made to feel like a stranger; someone who doesn't belong? Isn't it the responsibility of the host family to welcome the new addition with a lot of love and affection? After all, she does come from an entirely different environment, a place where the mindsets, way of speaking and ways of doings things may be slightly; and in some cases, majorly different! She walks in thinking that this is going to be her new home, but if she's constantly reminded that she comes from elsewhere, and that she needs to abide by a different set of rules, and that she is the daughter-in-law, how is she ever going to feel at home or a part of the new family? And since she is only the daughter-in-law, she needs to abide some really archaic and nonsensical rules like not sitting at the same height as others (she needs to sit at a lower height), not hum a tune in front of the father-in-law, then off course there is the dress code and worse still is that she isn't supposed to mix her laundry with the rest of the family. What I'm trying to get at is that if such laws; that have no real logic behind them, are imposed on a daughterin-law, how is she ever supposed to feel at home? And the best part is that there are many families that still believe in imposing such illogical and irrelevant laws even in this modern day and age.

(Why aren't such laws also applicable to the daughter and why only the daughter-in-law? Before a girl gets married, she has a name. However, once she enters the marital home, she loses that too and the elders begin addressing her as "Buwari"; meaning Daughter-in-law in Assamese.)

Although there are many that have understood, there are still countless others out there who resort to such practices even today. I don't wish to prove anyone wrong, however, why should anyone follow such illogical and nonsensical practices that can actually harm a family? There are times when such fickle things can break a budding relationship.

Who was responsible to help me not get pregnant at such a tender age? Why didn't the elders in the family take the onus to make sure that I didn't have to suffer the pangs of pregnancy when I was still underage? Was it right in the first place to get me married off at that age? From just a daughter and a sister, I suddenly became a wife, a daughter-in-law to some, sister-in-law to others, and in some cases, even an aunt or a grandmother. Just because of a societal norm, I was suddenly supposed to become much older than my real age. Along with the roles, I was suddenly entrusted with the responsibilities of an elder, even though I hadn't matured enough. Was it right on the behalf of the elders who I so trusted to make me forcibly accept this dramatic change in my life?

I took it on, as a challenge of sorts. I was also scared to rebel. I was still very young and didn't know anything. But then again, why did the elders who were supposed to know everything decide to turn a Nelson's eye to my plight? Why did they willingly refuse to understand and remain in a state of denial? Was it that they were very tightly ensconced in their illogical beliefs just because they lacked a proper education, and blindly believed anything in the name of cultural and traditional values?

Chapter 2
Page 7

If I look at things from their point of view, I suppose I didn't meet up to their expectations. Although, I didn't promise them anything, the truth is that I tried my level best to do everything that would make them happy. Maybe they weren't very happy about the fact that I wanted to study, or maybe they just felt disrespected because I wore Kurta-Pyjamas to college. Then again, why should what I wear, especially at a place that demanded that I wear it, be held against me? I know that I didn't wear clothes that would reveal much or anything that wasn't socially acceptable. As a daughter or even as a daughter-in-law, perhaps I wasn't as highly educated. Neither did I learn how to fulfill the responsibilities of a homemaker. No one really taught me; and especially because I got married off all of a sudden without any real planning. Maybe I couldn't be the daughter-in-law that they were looking for because of my age disadvantage. However, deep inside, I knew that I always gave it my best shot and tried to be all that they wanted me to be if not more.

I have always wanted to ask them this question. Not just them, but to everyone at large. Would people prefer a daughter-in-law who adhered to the dress code; donned a Mekhela-Sador, covered her hair and all the outwardly makings of a perfect daughter-in-law while she constantly ill treated them and cursed them from within; or would a daughter-in-law who wore clothes that she was comfortable in, gave everyone their due respect and did her best to keep everyone happy and contented be more acceptable?

There are many times when a home breaks up because of the dogmatic beliefs and ego of a few. How is a relationship to be built when beliefs in illogical and nonsensical cultural practices outweigh the relationship itself? I don't think that it's written anywhere that only a proper dress code and the ability to do household chores make a good wife or daughter-in-law.

Chapter 2
Page 8

The days passed, the pregnancy progressed. Everything seemed to be going well; the love that I received from my husband, and the care and attention that I received from everyone around left me nothing much to complain about. Yet I was uneasy. I still felt that things could have been better. I suppose it had something to do with the fact that my husband still wanted his sexual desires fulfilled by me even in that phase of pregnancy. I felt like I was being taken undue advantage of and maybe even abused. Neither could I refuse him, nor did he ever care to ask if I was okay with having sex then. Having good friends can be a blessing and benefits in many ways. Yet, implementing advice; however good the intention may be, from ill-informed friends can do just the opposite; more harm than good. And some such friends advised my husband to continue to maintain sexual relations with me even through the pregnancy. Their justification was that if he maintained sexual relations with me even when I was carrying would only strengthen the husband-wife bond and that I would be healthier. I believe that he definitely meant well for the two of us, however inane that advice may have been.

I was really disturbed; physically, mentally and emotionally. I had no one to talk to. Since I didn't have a really outgoing type of personality, I didn't have any close friends with whom I could share my pain and thoughts with. In addition to that almost all my ties with my school friends had been severed by then too. My husband would drop me off to college and pick me back up once classes were over. I wasn't allowed to socialize with any of my classmates. Whatever I did or wherever I went I had to be accompanied by my husband. I would get whatever I wanted; dresses, food and all that a girl can want; so long as it was within reach. Despite that I felt incomplete. To me it felt like, as a wife, my sole objective was to keep my husband sexually satisfied; something that was killing me inside very slowly. Deep within I was hurting so much and since there was no way for me to let it out, I would start picking arguments over really silly things. There was nothing else that I could do besides crying, throw tantrums and get into unnecessary fights with my husband.

Even my relationship with my parents and siblings seemed to be drifting away. I couldn't even speak freely over the phone because there was always someone or the other around. I didn't have a personal mobile phone yet; something that I could use to speak with from the privacy of my own space. And maybe I also took my father's parting advice a little too seriously. I kept being patient, didn't speak ill of my in-laws, and I tried to be as fluid as water could be. I would always behave and do things exactly the way my in-laws wanted them to be. There were many arguments and the relationship wasn't exactly a bed of roses. But I still tried my level best to show my husband the respect that was due and in fact, even tried to force myself to actually love him.

And in the midst of all of this, there was always the issue of me going to college and the kind of dress that I wore to college. Since this decision was more of a compromise situation for my in-laws, they weren't really happy. And that affected the environment at home too. I still remember the day when one of my mother-in-law's relatives called her and asked about me in the course of the conversation. Since I was sitting right next to my mother-in-law I actually overheard her telling the relative very acerbically, "Yes, I did get a daughter-in-law thinking that she would take care of me from now on and that I would be allowed to relax at home. But the tables have turned and it's me who's taking care of her since she goes to college now". She said what she did loud enough for me to hear. What I'd like to know is why is a daughter going to college any different from a daughter-in-law going to one? Why isn't a daughter-in-law given the same kind of love and support that a daughter would get? Why this mindset even in a progressive world like today's?

I had this Mahi; what we call a mother's younger sister in Assamese, visit us one day. She was actually my mother-in-law's younger sister. I knew that she loved me a lot and somehow I always felt that her love was a lot more refreshing. Maybe because she didn't attach any strings to the love she showed me. She decided to stay for lunch. I was in the kitchen preparing the lunch while everyone else was in the verandah chatting. She walked into the kitchen to see what I was doing and started enquiring about me in general. She was looking at me generally when her eyes fell on my feet. In utter shock, she immediately rushed me out of the kitchen and lay me down in my bed. She noticed that both my feet were heavily swollen. She not only lay me down, but she immediately started to also massage my feet and asked me to take rest and not do any work. I still remember the look on her face. She was really disturbed and seemed like she was under some kind of tremendous pressure. I also remember overhearing her arguing with my in-laws while I was still in bed. "She's pregnant! Why are you making her slog like that the whole day? She's still a little girl and she's carrying a child just so that you can extend your family line. What will you do if there are any complications and what you're doing just isn't right" is what I overheard her saying. But my in-laws just wouldn't back down. My mother-in-law's argument was that she had birthed 5 children and despite her pregnancies, she would still do all the household chores; in fact, a lot more than I ever did. My Mahi's arguments that the old days were different considering that the quality of food and the environment weren't as polluted and were definitely healthier than today's. But all her arguments fell on deaf ears.

I still remember all that Mahi said that day; also the fact that, at least she played my advocate and argued against her own elder sister. There was someone who actually pointed out my in-law's wrongs and perhaps that's why I begin to respect Mahi all the more. Or, maybe it was because, during those trying times, she was the only one who stood by me, understood and spoke of my pain.

There are still arguments over trivial matters between a daughter-in-law and a mother-in-law. The root cause of most of the arguments; if you observe them minutely, are based on ego. In many cases a mother-in-law finds it very difficult to accept that the daughter-in-law has a slightly more comfortable life than she did. What do you think is more important; love, affection and kindness, or strict adherence to list of inane, obsolete and illogical cultural practices? You be the judge.

Chapter 2
Page 9

Life went on with its usual ups and downs. After all, not everyone thinks alike. My pregnancy advanced even further and people started discussing if it'll be a boy or a girl. Everyone wanted a boy, but I guess everyone forgot that I wasn't the one to decide what the child will be. With all the discussions, I began to doubt myself and wonder if I'd be held responsible if I didn't give birth to a male. And that's why whenever I prayed, I asked God for a boy and not a girl. I would make deals with God and observe various rituals just so that God would hear my pleas and bless me with a boy child. I was under tremendous pressure from my in-laws to give birth to a male child; as though I had any choice in the matter. Everyone would keep harping about the benefits of having a male child. I was also reminded continuously about how dejected my father-in-law would be if I gave birth to a girl instead of a boy. And to do this, they'd always bring up the topic about how sad they were when their own daughter gave birth to a girl. This just made me even more fearful and I was frightened that if I were to give birth to a girl, my father-in-law just wouldn't accept her.

And all this happened not because the people around me were uneducated; in fact, my husband and my brothers-in law were pretty well qualified academically. The main factor here was ignorance. I was a small town girl who hadn't completed her formal education as yet, however, the ones that were from the city and educated willingly chose to remain uninformed and ignorant. Such was the level of ignorance that my husband didn't even stop to think twice about how this could have an adverse effect on my state of mind and also the pregnancy.

Not many seem to understand how such things can actually help break up families and relationships. Is it possible for a nation to progress if most people harbor such narrow mentality? What example is the older generation setting for the younger? Isn't it time that the older generation start changing their thought process, get rid of their narrow mindedness and lead by example? Or is it that they want to continue down this path till every home is broken or disturbed? Yes, I understand that many from the older generation lacked the kind of education that was really required; while some are so thick headed that they just refuse to yield to some of their inane beliefs. However, isn't it the responsibility of the educated to rise above such thought processes and try and get some of the older ones to join them too? Although my husband and his brothers were all students of science when in college, they just didn't have it in them to apply their learning practically. And just because they didn't have it in them to get their parents to see the folly of their thinking, I continued to suffer. I did point this out on one of my earlier chapters that we are taught to respect our elders and obey them without any questions because the elders always know best. But is that really true? And if it is, on what authority can one say that the elders can never be wrong? Why couldn't my husband or his brothers make their parents point out the wrong that they were doing? In retrospect I regret that I was being absolutely unjust; not just to myself, but also that little new life that was blossoming in my womb.

There are still many cases even in this day and age; especially in this country, where a daughter-in-law is tortured if the in-laws get to know that she's carrying a girl's life in the womb; in fact there are also many cases of forced abortions.

The situation had in fact come to such that prenatal sex determination has been made a punishable crime in the country. The worst case is if she were to give birth to a baby girl at the end of it all. There are countless cases of female babies being abandoned on the streets, or dumped into public trash cans. And I know it sounds heartless, but with the kind of torture that the girl child has to undergo through life, the ones that are killed at birth are certainly lucky. Gender discrimination is still a hard reality right from the time of conception.

There are about 33 million Gods in Hinduism, including many Goddesses. Some of the most famous ones that are worshipped are Maa Durga, Maa Kali, Maa Saraswati and Maa Laxmi. In fact, there are many famous temples and events that are dedicated to honour the various Goddesses across the country. People observe fasting rituals for 10 days prior to Durga Puja, then there's the famous Vaishno Devi Temple in Jammu where people undertake and arduous trek uphill, the Kamakhya temple in Guwahati that is known for its animal sacrifice rituals and many more. The one thing common and ironic at the same time is that most people that visit these temples of Goddesses beg that they be blessed with a male child.

Are the Goddesses supposed to be happy with such prayers; such requests? After all, you're asking a lady God not to grant a boon for a girl! Sounds ironical, doesn't it? Is this what devotion is all about; acting as if you're the humblest person on earth and then you start discriminating between the genders? How does this even make any sense? Why is girl child still killed? Why is woman tortured or disowned for giving birth to a girl? Why has the mechanism been so ineffective to stop such practices despite the stringent laws already in place? Or should the educators take the blame for failing to teach people to stop gender based discrimination?

The government or the educators aren't to be blamed entirely. Unless society at large stops believing such stupidity about the superiority of the male child, this country will never progress. It's high time that educators and social workers work harder; especially with people that still manifest such obsolete thinking patterns. And unless we do this, do you really think we will be actually paying obeisance to the Goddesses?

Chapter 2
Page 10

I desperately wanted to speak with my parents; tell them everything that I was going through, instead, my mind was a complete blank since I was so completely engrossed in fulfilling my duties as a wife and a daughter-in-law. I didn't know where to start and how to end since I didn't have a complete understanding of my innermost feelings. All I knew is that things weren't what they seemed and that I was doing many things only by force; almost always unwillingly. I started creating a world of my own; one where I was mature and understanding despite my age. There was no one I could call a friend. Even though I went to college, most of my peers avoided me for two main reasons; one was that I was married and secondly, they came to know about the restrictions that were imposed on me. And I'm sure you know how word spreads in a college. I was never invited to their gatherings, asked out for movies or shopping; all-in-all, I was never made to feel a part of. I would feel even lonelier when I would see my college mates; people in the same age group as I was, enjoy life freely. I was hurt, I so longed to be free myself; do the things I wanted to do, enjoy the way almost all other teens do, explore life through a teenager's and college student's eyes. And even the ones that did speak with me; albeit very guardedly, were very curious about why I married so early in life. I would mostly beat around the bush and never give them a concrete answer; and that's perhaps because even I didn't know why. What attracted a lot of surprise and sympathy was when they got to know about the age gap of 16 years between my husband and me. And that's what made me clam up even more and would try and avoid speaking about the age gap; more out of shame and anything else.

14th of December, 2005; my first child was born. Most women remember the joy of bringing on the first born and don't remember the pain much. I, on the other hand, join the many that remembers the pain only. I was just 17 and we were still in the 1st year of our marriage. Given my age and my girth, the gynecologist advised against a C-Section and preferred a normal delivery. I had gone to the hospital for a regular check-up and was admitted that very day. My mother was with me while my husband was at home. At about 11 that night while I was playing a video game, I felt a sudden pain. I rushed to the washroom with my mother in tow. All I knew was that I was about to give birth but didn't know what to do or what would happen. The labour pains began to intensify and I was crying out in pain. The doctor rushed to me, checked me up and said that I would have to wait and bear the pain a little longer. By now I wasn't just crying, but kicking up a ruckus at the hospital. I was administered a bottle of saline water which I thought was to replace the fluids I was losing. However, it turned out that it was more a support for the baby in the womb. I remember tearing out the needle from my arm in anger from all the pain. No one could control the ruckus I was creating. In fact, even the nursing staff began to question my mother and my husband about the logic behind making a child like me bear the pangs of delivery. I stayed like that for almost 5 to hours till about 4 in the morning. When I was just about lose all consciousness from the pain, the doctor finally decided to do a C-Sec. I woke a long time after the little one was delivered. I felt absolutely drained and didn't have an ounce of energy. All I remember is feeling my mother's hand on my head gently rubbing it and I burst into tears. That's when I understood what my mother meant when she said, "You'll understand pain only when you give birth to the first one". And when I mentioned that to her she said very apologetically, "I made a big mistake. I shouldn't have gotten you married off so early."

So, that's how my first child was born; and it was a boy. My mother stayed back with me for a long time even after he was born. Despite that, I just couldn't bring myself around to revealing what I was going through and what I was feeling. Perhaps I had subconsciously accepted my fate.

The surprising part is that I started to get jealous of my own new born child. Whenever he got all the attention;

which by any means any new born usually does, I would burn with envy. I addition to that I was battling a whole lot of other effects brought on by the usual hormonal changes that a mother goes through. Unlike a mother, I would get angry and irritated whenever he was made to suckle. I hated it, and what I also detested was when I would start to lactate without any reason.

As the days went along, I felt my responsibilities rising. I was lost again and had lost track of almost everything. I felt like I went through the day in a daze. The constant pressure from the in-laws and the regular tiffs with the husband didn't help make things any better. The persistent pressure to complete the household chores, taking care of the baby, and then there were always the sexual gratification requests from the husband. Things had come to such that I had begun contemplating suicide to try and get to a better place; if there was any. To make matters worse, there was the constant nagging by the in-laws to not attend the 1st year final exams since there was a new born baby at home now. Despite all of that I just hung in there and refused to give up.

After the exams, I went back to my mother's house. I stayed there for a while. That's when I found out that my husband was going through a financial crisis owing to losses in his business. I really didn't understand how I could help despite me really wanting to. I would call him to try and offer some solace, however he'd either ignore my calls or even if he did answer, he was usually very curt and at times, even bordering on rude. There were also times when my mother-in-law would answer my husband's calls. And when she did, she would not lose the opportunity to make her displeasure known, berate me or make me feel guilty for not being with my husband at times like these. Maybe she was absolutely right from her perspective of things. After all, a loving and dutiful wife ought to stand by her husband; especially during the tough times. But, I just didn't know what I was supposed to do and there was no one there to actually guide me. Despite all that suffering, I did not divulge anything to my parents.

My husband came home one day to meet me. I sulked and refused to talk to him properly for treating me the way he did whenever I called. That night we had a major argument. My bones of contention were his allowing his mother to receive my calls, for not explaining things to me directly and telling me what he expected out of me. All my days of bottled up grief and anger just came flowing out like water from a dam burst. I cried to him, but he just refused to understand my points of view. Perhaps it was the age gap. I was so angry that I finally asked him to do one of the most unrealistic and stupidest things a good wife can do; to choose between his mother and me. I realized my folly the moment the words left my mouth. However, all I wanted him to do actually is profess that he truly loved me; that's all. He was speechless for a while. Maybe he didn't know what he was supposed to say without lying or upsetting me. All I wanted though is for him to apologize for treating me the way he did and to promise that he wouldn't allow any third person to interfere in our misunderstandings; just like how I didn't say anything to my parents. He then said that he loved both of us and could not leave anyone. But I was so possessive about him that his answer offended me. It came to my mind at once that if he could ask for his sexual need gratification the moment he met me, why couldn't he answer a simple question; letting his ego down for a bit. It was like professing his love for me was the hardest thing in the world, or was completely against his ethics. His silence was deafening and I lost any and all semblance of sanity and decided that I must end it all for good. I lit myself on fire. To date, I don't know what happened exactly and I can feel the shivers go down my spine as I write this part of my story. I am so petrified even today that I can't even stand burning scenes in the movies and usually stop watching the movie if it contains any such act.

I was admitted to an ICU with 45% burn injuries. I was in tremendous pain again. In spite of all that happened, my husband refused to visit me at the hospital. Maybe his ego and his pride wouldn't allow him to come see me. My dad, however, stayed by me all the while. He cried continuously and that's when he finally asked me the question that I had wanted to hear so desperately for so long; "What was going on? Why didn't you say anything?"

Chapter 2
Page 11

The husband came along with the doctor to visit me the next day and said that I would have to remain in the ICU for at least a month. My family managed to convince the doctor and hush up the entire incident. The burns extended from my chest right down to the thighs and I was in a tremendous amount of pain and agony. My mother brought my son for me to see after about 2 days. He was about 6 months old then. I tried to suckle him, but found that I had dried up. Maybe it was because of the heavy medication that I was on. I would look at that poor innocent little life trying his best to drink whatever he could find. After all it was his mother's milk. I had lost all sense of any self worth that remained and began detesting myself all the more. What was this little innocent one's fault? Why did he have to suffer because I couldn't get a handle on my life; because I couldn't give him a healthy and homely environment to grow into? Just because I couldn't accept and live life or fight against what I thought was wrong, wasn't I making this little child suffer unnecessarily? My mother eventually found other sources to feed the child; however, he suffered for no fault of his.

My in-laws came to visit me at the hospital. To date I am not sure if they meant well or were just plain uncaring about my plight. All they were grateful about is that the incident didn't attract any kind of media attention or that it did not happen in Guwahati. They were only glad that they did not get implicated in this in any way. After the visit, they went straight to their daughter's place. They didn't even bother to call on my mother or take a look at my child; their grandson. My mother, on the other hand assumed all responsibilities; bringing me my meals, taking care of my son, and the usual household chores that needed to be done every day. How I wished that my in-laws would help my mother out, even if it was a little bit. After all, they were the ones who pressurized me into giving them a grandchild. But they just didn't seem to care.

My burns began to heal eventually and I was moved to a normal hospital room. The bandages that covered me came off and I got to see the actual state that I was in only then. What I saw frightened me and sent me further in the realms of depressions. There were times when the injuries would give out a bad smell and I would feel disgusted. My fair colored skin had turned into a ghastly mix of red and black. Some of those scars still remain as a ghastly reminder of my life's suffering.

A few things happened inside the hospital room too, which had been very traumatic for me. But I could not resist my husband from being insensitive towards me.

Even through the pain and the suffering, I thought that; as a wife he had all the right over my body and I had none.

I was discharged from the hospital after about 3 months. I saw myself completely after a long time. I couldn't stand straight since I was mostly curled up owing to the pain and the bandages. I couldn't turn around to take a look at my back even in the mirror. And when I did see the front, I was in complete shock. Perhaps I paid the price for being a little too proud of my skin colour. Now I was absolutely disgusted with my own body.

A few months later, my husband started on a project. Since it was easier for him to commute to the project site, we moved to his elder sister's place. This was the same sister whose son had also started going to college when I did. After a long time I found some amount of happiness and started to think that things will now look up from now on. This was when our 1st year final exam results were declared. In fact even this sister's daughter's results were declared on the same day. In anticipation of the results, a feast had been organized. Almost all Assamese traditional celebratory feasts usually have duck meat and fish on the menu.

I scored well, considering the circumstances that I studied under. However, that happiness that I felt for a while soon came to an end. The feast was called off. Why? My husband's niece and nephew couldn't clear the exams and the entire environment in the house turned gloomy. What hurt me more is that no one even bothered to take my results into consideration and even offer a sweet; as is traditionally the thing to do. I understood that the niece and the nephew not doing well was a matter of concern. However, wasn't I a part of the family too? Why was I treated so differently? Shouldn't my hard work and scores have mattered to anyone at all? What was my fault in all of this? Was it only because I wasn't born into the family? The strange thing is that this happens very commonly; not just with the daughterin-law, but even with daughters in many cases across the country.

A few days later I went back to my mother's place and stayed there even longer. I suppose I had to stay there long mainly because my husband was still not out of the financial mess and he couldn't afford to bring me back to his place. Since looking after the little one and me was going to be difficult, he preferred that we stay at my mother's.

The days went by and admissions to the 2nd year of college had begun. No one, however, showed any concern about getting me admitted to the next session. Perhaps my academic progress hardly mattered since I was already married and no one saw any value in furthering my studies. There was just no support from anyone.

In addition to all of that, I had become a victim to neighborhood gossip. My parents overheard people mentioning that I was either separated or divorced from my husband since I had been at my mother's for so long. The suicide attempt didn't help make matters any better. My parents were very worried. Their reputation was at stake. I couldn't even tell my parents about the losses in business and the financial worries that my husband was going through. Not finding any other way, I called my husband to take me back to Guwahati with the excuse that society wouldn't understand my staying at my mother's place for so long. He finally agreed and took me back. Despite all of this I didn't mention anything about my husband's state of affairs to my parents.

Why? Why did things have to come to such? People blamed me for the suicide attempt, said that it was a very bad move; and maybe even rightly so. However, did anyone bother to even find out why I did so? Did anyone try and find out what I was going through; mentally, emotionally, physically? Why didn't anyone try and find out why that girl who loved herself, who was proud of her image and looks actually try to destroy herself? Was anyone really concerned at all, or was it just superficial care? Maybe no one understood, or care to understand at all. Maybe even I didn't understand exactly what was going on and was unnecessarily ashamed of myself and my actions. I would hear people talk and began feeling like a criminal who tried to take a life. I also felt guilty about all the problems that I caused everyone; my husband, my parents, and my in-laws especially.

I was just 17 and had still not been able to figure out what was the right thing to do and what was wrong. Like all other teens, I was mostly led by emotional impulse. If I would have been able to differentiate between right and wrong, maybe I wouldn't even have gotten married. After all, who wants to knowingly spoil their lives? I would seriously like to know how many people actually hate themselves so much that they want to take their own lives? I'm sure not many people hate themselves so much. The ones that do try or take their own lives usually; like me, do it because they find no other way to escape the pain; not because they hate themselves. Maybe I had lost all hope because of the mental fatigue, depression and trauma that I had to live every day. Maybe the only way I saw to escape from the ring was by throwing in the towel.

Why is it that, even today, a husband's rights and wants override those of the wife's? Why doesn't a husband have to seek permission before asking the wife to do anything? Why does the wife have to be treated like some kind of personal property to be dealt with in any way the husband thinks fit? Why can't most men let their egos and their pride down and show a little more love, concern and respect to the wife? After all, most women leave almost everything and does all that is needed to adjust and live a happy life with the husband. It's a definite possibility that a proper lack of knowledge and education leads to all of this. And then there's always the dogma attached to a patriarchal society; one that says that the man is always right. Who's actually responsible to break such beliefs? Doesn't that change start with us?

Why didn't anyone think me to be a part of the family on the day the results were declared? Why didn't anyone think that even I might have some kind of expectations? I agree, I was married and I was also a mother. However, the fact remains that I was still a teenager; and that too, a college going one who had dreams and ambitions of her own. Why wasn't I treated like one of their own children? Or were they just incapable of thinking that way? Although I was in the same age category of my husband's niece and nephew, did I lose the privilege to be treated like them just because I was married and a mother to a child? In fact, shouldn't I have been appreciated for studying and clearing the exams without any real support despite the roles and responsibilities that I had; as a newly wedded wife, a daughter-law, and most of all, a new mother? Or was I not entitled to even that much love and concern?

Why did it also feel like even my parents had disowned me, didn't care about what I was going through? Why didn't they bother finding out more about me? Why didn't they ever ask if I was happy; happy with their decision, content with my new environment? Why didn't they ask if I've been able to adjust to the environment that they put in? Why were my parents more bothered about what society thought instead of being concerned about the well-being of their own child?

*Dear society! Maybe you've gotten into the habit of imposing such laws and ethics that actually hurt a person more than making them feel wanted. Maybe some of those laws; written or unsaid, are actually inane and shouldn't even apply. Yes, some of these so called laws and ethics are also archaic and illogical which aren't supposed to exist anymore. Yes, laws are a necessity, however they must be disbanded once they've served the purpose and as time changes. Some of these laws and ethics of conduct not only hurt us adults, but also have a ripple effect on the generations to follow. *

I didn't commit any crime; that's what I know. My biggest crime though, according to this society is that I was born a girl. I didn't want to bother anyone with my worries. I only wanted to adjust; to fit in. I bottled it all up. Maybe I was one of the lucky ones who managed to survive; unlike the many that finding no way out of the pain decide take matters into their own hands and end it all. Then there are those who live through the pain and eventually degrade mentally, physically and emotionally. With these unsaid, illogical, and mostly idiotic codes of ethics that most societies abide by; aren't they the ones that are actually committing the crime? Aren't they the ones that are actually ruining the future for the generations to come? Isn't it high time we look deep within and stopped knowingly or unknowingly hurting others with our unjustifiable and illogical codes that we force down their throats?

Chapter 2
Page 12

It was like I had begun a new life after coming back to Guwahati. My responsibilities had definitely increased. Looking after the child, taking care of the home without allowing my husband to be distracted from his work; I took all the responsibilities on head long. Eventually I also started to lend a helping hand in his business. Even if I didn't want it, I had begun to learn the ropes of taking care of a home. In the midst of all of this, I dropped out of college; in fact I didn't even get myself admitted to the 2nd term. Somewhere down the line, around this time, as per my father-in-law's suggestion, my husband, my child and I moved out and began living separately from his family. We took up our own place. It actually felt like I had finally matured into a complete woman.

As with establishing all new businesses, we too had our share of financial hard times. I still remember those days when I would collect loose change to buy the essentials. But, I wouldn't bother my husband with all that lest he get distracted from his work. I tried to be the perfect wife to my husband, a perfect mother to my child and a perfect businesswoman. In all of this, I lost the real me; my idea of the ideal woman.

Finally the business started to yield returns and grow. It did have its ups and downs, but by now there were more ups then downs. In between all of this, in 2009, I got myself admitted to the 2nd year of college. Even through all of our own problems, I would always be there for my in-laws. From taking my parents-in-law to the hospital, being with them through sickness, advising the nieces and the nephews, I did everything with a major degree of success. It seemed as though I was the perfect wife, daughter-inlaw, sister-in-law and all the other relationships that one can name. However, there was still that nagging feeling of being less than. Although I derived all my happiness from making my husband and his family happy, I wasn't content with who I was. Somewhere down the line I had lost the real me and I didn't quite like that.

Maybe my concern over my husband's well being; his happiness, satisfying each and every one of his needs took a toll on my health. I started to suffer with a lot of hormone related issues which would again keep me depressed for long periods. Owing to all the health issues that I was going through, I began skipping the contraceptive tablets; not because I wanted to, but because I forget to take them. We tried many other methods of contraception like the Copper T and different kinds of injections. However, my health kept deteriorating and eventually the doctor advised against the usage of any kind of contraceptive methods. And from then on, there was spurt in my cases of abortions. Even then, my husband just refused to understand; or was it that he just didn't care enough?

I was either scared of my husband because he was older than I was, or I had bought into the concept of "a husband is always right and should be respected and obeyed at all times" hook, line and sinker. And because of this, I couldn't be absolutely open with him no matter how much I wanted it or however much I tried. Although my husband made sure that all the necessities were provided in addition to anything that made me happy, I was still not allowed to go out anywhere; either alone or with anyone else. Wherever I went or wanted to go, I would always have to be accompanied by my husband. I failed to understand why that was. Why wasn't I allowed to be a little more independent? Was it that he was a little overprotective because of my age, or was it that he was absolutely obsessed? Let's not also negate the possibility that he did not trust me.

I never went against him. Perhaps that was because I thought the whole world of him. Yes, we had our ups and downs, our share of arguments, but I never refused him anything. So long as he was happy. I never thought that I would not be able to handle his behavior or satisfy his sexual needs; maybe that was because he really loved me and took good care of me. I couldn't even bring myself to dislike him, much less hate him. It was like I was beginning to grow up around him and from a teenager, soon became an adult. And when I turned 18, we got officially married in a court of law. This happened somewhere in the year 2010. I was about 20 years old then. Despite being married for close to 4 years and all the struggles that we had been through together, my husband still seemed quite confused about our relationship or maybe he was just a bit too over conscious. He had a very stromg belief in astrology and would consult various astrologers. One such astrologer told my husband one day that I was a "Mangalik" and since he had married me, he would die soon. According to Hindu astrology, a "Mangalik: person is born under the influence of Mars and is considered to carry some defects associated with the planet. Superstition has it that a Managalik a Non-Managalik can have disastrous effects, usually ending with the untimely death of the Non-Mangalik Person. And I suppose it was just my luck that the moment my husband heard that, he decided to divorce me; at least until a time when my stars aligned and worked in our favour again. Until then, he suggested that we live apart and that he would marry me only after my luck had changed. Between my tears of fright and frustration, I tried my best to convince my husband to get a second opinion. One of my cousins suggested another astrologer, however, my husband just wasn't satisfied with his readings and we finally decided to set out for Benares where the Hindu Almanac is mostly written.

He finally believed what that astrologer said and I escaped the divorcee tag. I started to feel so scared and guilty about everything that I began observing "Karwachot" a day when a wife observes a day long fast for her husband's well being and a long life. I also began observing many other rituals that could perhaps further my husband's well being.

In retrospect however, I wonder what my fault in all of this was. Why was I made to suffer for no fault of mine? Why was I made to feel the pain alone? After all, wasn't it he who so desperately wanted to marry me despite my age and everything?

At an age when most girls explore life, find their freedom and have friends, I felt like I had been imprisoned. At an age when I was supposed to be studying and enjoying with friends, I had assumed the worldly responsibility of an adult woman. Girls my age were more worried about academics, grades and which college they would go to where as I was worried about family, children, business and running a house. But I suppose my diary was written somewhat different. I had already seen health problems; gynecological issues and the likes that required regular medication; problems that people normally face when they are in their 40's. And I was just 20. The frequent abortions didn't help my mental and physical condition much either; I began to deteriorate very fast.

In spite of all of that, why did my husband so quickly decide to believe the words of a stranger? Why was he so frightened of his life just because someone else said it; and that too based on nothing but superstition? Was I at fault? He was obstinate about marrying me when he did. Why did he decide to desert me so quickly despite all the promises that he made before and after we had just gotten married? Is there any justifiable reason for asking for a divorce after he marries me and I also bear him his child before I had even turned into a legal adult? Or was this the reward that my sacrifices deserved? Why does a woman always have to be the one to compromise and sacrifice after marriage? We still think that the right thing to do is for the woman to get married, assume the husband's last name, forget about freedom and pursuing hobbies, give up any academic or professional ambitions. Is that truly justifiable?

Chapter 2
Page 13

I began studying again in 2011. I also brought my little sister to live with us. I wanted to mould her with hope to fulfill some of my broken dreams through her. But, most of all, at least I had someone to call my own; someone that I could at least speak with and be myself. I was so damaged from deep within, so deeply disgusted with whatever had happened to me so far that whenever I heard or saw any underage girl getting married, I would be repulsed and get angry and at times, go back into a state of prolonged depression. In addition to that, I had begun to hide my husband's and my ages. This was mainly to avoid the look of surprise and shock on their faces and also to avoid the subsequent questions. I started to feel a great level of discomfort whenever anyone questioned me about our huge age gap in addition to feeling ashamed. In fact, even my husband had begun to feel that way whenever he was questioned; especially around his acquaintances. If you remember, in one of the earlier chapters I mentioned that I had begun helping him with his business. That's when I would have to meet some of the concerned people. The age gap was so obvious that people who met us for the first time would usually confuse us for a father and daughter.

Although I was quite friendly with my husband's friends, I was always very reserved at the same time. Somehow our thoughts and wave lengths didn't quite match. Also, mostly we didn't think alike. I would try really hard, but I suppose the age gaps were a definitely impeding factor. To think at their level, I'd have to act like them; which I did to a great extent of success. But deep within, I longed for that freedom of youth; to not have so many responsibilities, to fly like a free bird high up in the sky. But I just couldn't. I was stuck in that cycle of being the wife, the daughter-in-law and a mother and I had to carry myself with that elegance and grace of a lady. Even though I had learnt a lot, I felt like I knew nothing at times. I'd feel ashamed, guilty and jealous at the same time whenever I saw people my age living their lives. The worst was that even when I did meet people my age, I couldn't bring myself to behave like them and also that I noticed that I had started thinking differently from them. Not being able to match up with people of my age or even the ones that were older just drove me further into a feeling of loneliness and solitude.

Around this time I started to develop a strong feeling that there was some great injustice that had been done to me. I felt like I wasn't being true to myself. It was like I was maintaining this relationship just for the sake of it and that I had been shortchanging myself all the while. I wanted to tell my husband all that I was feeling, vent out all my frustration, but I was scared and didn't really believe that he would be able to look at things from my point of view. I was sick and tired of living a life that seemed like a prison sentence, I longed for freedom. I had had enough of acting like I loved him anymore. Just the thought that I was stuck with him despite the fact that I didn't love him pained me all the more. However, I continued to fake it thinking that maybe someday he'll change and he'll actually begin to love me for who I truly was. I would see other couples and feel even more saddened. Even I would've loved going out on long drives, have candle lit dinners, go on dates; mainly, I wanted some form of romance. It's just that he wasn't at all a person like that. Perhaps it was the age gap that created the clash of thoughts and expectations. I still didn't lose hope. I tried organizing dinners at home and setting up dates like most young couples would. I thought at least those things would make me happy and that things could get back to normal. Even that didn't seem to work. Maybe it was his age, because he just couldn't do the things I wanted or be who I wanted him to be. And the thought of ending the relationship grew even stronger each time I failed at these attempts of reconciliation. That's also when I realized that I hadn't volunteered or even accepted to become a part of this world; my husband's world. And the feeling to move out and live in a world of my own just grew stronger. The downside is that I had also begun to think and believe that

I really didn't have any right or say in the matter. And this conundrum is what became of my life.

My health started to deteriorate even more rapidly. I became a frequent visitor to a few hospitals in Delhi. Lumps like formations on the breast, irregular menstrual cycles and cysts in the ovaries became my major health concerns. Even the doctors advised that conceiving another child could prove to be hazardous. Besides restrictions on my diet and a whole lot of medicines, I had to keep going in for regular check-ups. I was mostly overstressed and depressed, despite which my husband just seemed to be absolutely nonchalant and didn't exercise any form of self restraint or care.

Soon my son too started schooling. Taking care of the house, extra care of the child since he also suffered from asthma, my studies took the hit once again and I stopped. I started a small business of my own and the involvement managed to help me escape from the hurt and the pain that I was going through. Once I started working, I found that I now had a semblance of freedom. I was allowed to go out whenever I wanted and could go to the movies and shopping without my husband in tow. It was such a pleasure. My husband did promise that I would be allowed to take my own decisions once I turned 22 and he kept to his word and became a lot more flexible.

I wanted to feel what it was like to be an expectant mother once again. After all when I was with the first child, I was still too young to fully comprehend and enjoy the being pregnant. My son was already 7 years old by then and my husband was also getting on in age. Even my parents suggested that we have another child. We decided it would be best for me to try conceiving only under a doctor's expert guidance. However, there were a series of miscarriages owing to all the health issues that I faced from earlier. Eventually, I did conceive and I just couldn't express how happy I was. Despite all the care that I had to exercise and the restrictions that I had to maintain, I was truly happy and enjoyed being pregnant this time around. Even my husband started to take extra care of me and did exactly what the doctor suggested. He tried his best at all times to see to it that I was happy and content and this time he didn't even make any sexual advances. November of 2012; and a new life came out of my womb; a girl; and I was even happier; after all only I knew the value of a girl.

Two children to take care of in addition to taking care of my husband, the household chores, and my son's studies, I began to study again to complete my graduation and also started my own designer line of clothes. Even though I was still filled with negativity and hopelessness, I decided not to give up and worked consistently to fulfill my dreams. Even through all of this, I finally managed to graduate and fulfill one of my life's major ambitions.

One day, sometime in 2013, all that I had faced in the past caught up with me; the abuse and the injustice. My husband had pressurized me for sex that day. Not only was I not in the mood, but also being the mother of a girl I just couldn't bear it anymore and I broke my years of silence and the dam burst wide open. The trigger point was when my husband used an expletive and also pointed out that I was frigid just because he couldn't handle my refusal. I couldn't take it anymore and pushing him away with whatever strength I had, started to abuse him.

I told him everything. Right from what happened during the childhood right up till the present. There was nothing stopping me. All the years of pent up anger, frustration and shame; all blurted out in just one night. I also told him that I detested sex in any form and that I would prefer if he sought my permission even before touching me. I also asked him if he didn't understand why I always went into a bad mood or fought with him every time we had sex. I broke down every incident that happened with me during my childhood in detail; just as I have in this book. I let him know that I didn't have a childhood with fairies and elves; instead I had one that was filled with goblins and monsters.

I also asked him if he was ready to still accept me despite all that I had told him. And if he agreed, he would also have to give me my space, allow me to treat my body as my own and that he'd have to give me my due respect and love me without any conditions. He wouldn't be allowed to treat me as his personal property to do with me as and how he pleases. I let him know that if he wasn't willing to abide by those conditions, I'd have be left with no other alternative than leaving him. It was a bolt from the blue for him and he just sat rooted to where he was like a statue.

After I told him all that, I walked out of the room and the first thing I did was to call my mother and told her all that I told my husband. I realized that I had been crying and shouting while speaking with my mother and I suppose, in retrospect, that it was more out of relief than anger. My mother listened to me and asked me why I hadn't told her all along. And I told her the truth. I told her that how scared I was; of her and of the situations, I also told her that she wasn't caring enough to try and understand what I was going through in the first place. She was sad, but what she said next was something that I least expected from a mother; especially one that really cares. She said very cynically and with a mark of utter disappointment, "You've done right my shaming me in front of your husband. What do you think he'll think of me now? And don't you understand that he will leave you now?" It was like she just nuked me without any warning. Now it was my turn to be dumbstruck. But I promised myself then and there that come what may, I will always take care of both my children and give them the love, respect and understanding that they deserve; something that I had missed out in as a child and have been missing out on right till this very moment.

My husband approached me the next morning and apologized. He hugged me tight and promised me that he would never bother or pester me for sex anymore. I was really elated deep within. I felt like I was the luckiest person alive on earth right at that moment and forgot all those years of pain, suffering and angst for the time. It was like those bad things never happened to me. Our relationship mended gradually and I started to love and respect him all the more. I felt like I had actually met the greatest person in the world; someone who I could actually call my life partner.

Chapter 2
Page 14

Although the days went by pretty peacefully, one thing is for sure; things never remain the same and I realized that there is never a permanent solution to anything.

About a year passed without any major incidents. In fact, there was a lot of love and affection among the two of us and we were happy with each other. I began to think that I had found the perfect life partner.

However, things started to go back to what they were. I started to feel hopeless once again. Although I tolerated everything, I started to develop suicidal tendencies and even attempted it a few times without much success. Maybe it was the thought of my children that kept me alive. I started to drink and smoke heavily and noticed that there was a paradigm shift in my lifestyle. I was almost always in a state of depression; it was like someone locked me in that cage and threw away the key. I started to isolate myself from my husband. I would try and discuss things with him many times. He would always make promises, but they turned out to be mostly empty. Maybe he hadn't realized the gravity of the situation then. Although the talks would mostly resolve many things, it seemed that he would always be in a state of denial whenever he had the need to fulfill his sexual urge. It was like he knew the reality but wasn't ready to accept it. And that was slowly killing me from within. Very soon, things came to a standstill between the two of us and we just wouldn't get along; maybe because I refused to sacrifice or give in to his demands.

Even though I had warned him many times, he seemed to ignore all the warnings. Whatever I had regained in terms of my health began to deteriorate once again. He also began to neglect my doctor's appointments. He would accompany me at times, but mostly I'd end up going alone. He would mostly forget, turn up late or put the blame on pressure at work. The doctor had warned about a lot of things, however he just didn't seem to be concerned; leave alone showing any. I would warn him about leaving him, and at times also tell him that he'd lose me for good to the four horsemen. I was absolutely unwell and mostly go through the day feeling absolutely weak and lifeless.

In 2016 I had the 10th abortion and by then I was physically almost finished. My uterus had become affected to a point where it was impossible to cure. It seemed like all treatment methods had been exhausted because nothing seemed to work for me anymore. I was menstruating continuously and when the bleeding just didn't stop, the doctor said that there was no way other than removing the uterus surgically. That was the turning point because that's when my husband realized how much he had neglected all these all the while and felt absolutely guilty. He cried and said he was sorry for ignoring the symptoms and not being adequately careful for so long for which I had to suffer so much.

It was very risky, yet we decided to go to Chennai to see if I could get treated. The doctor also warned us that if we neglected this any further it'll only get worse and could also be the cause of my untimely death. The doctors in Chennai did manage to find some solutions which had a possibility of working. At the same time the doctors also berated my husband for neglecting this issue for so long. They told him that he was unknowingly playing with my life. This made him feel even more regretful and guilty and so he turned very caring.

I was admitted to Apollo Hospitals in Chennai and my treatment started almost immediately. They tried different types of medicines and procedures and finally narrowed down to the one that worked best. There was a form of treatment that was akin to chemotherapy for the next 3 months. They also administered some kind of an injection every week for those 3 weeks. My skin began to turn dry, my hair started to fall. The procedures were very painful and I suffered a lot. But I didn't want to give up. Somewhere deep within, I wanted to live life again. I regretted all the mistakes I made, I began to ask myself why couldn't I have loved myself more and not hurt myself so much. I began to look back at my life and wonder why was I so scared and allowed myself to be treated like a doormat all my life. Why did I allow people to dictate how I should be living my life? Why couldn't I be more confident and self-assertive? Why did I have to sacrifice so much all along that I had to suffer this pain and trauma today?

While I was undergoing my treatment in Chennai, I spoke with my elder brother one day. He suggested that I try and pick up a skill set while I was in the city. His suggestion made sense and even in between such painful treatment I decided to take up a course on cosmetology. I completed the course and I managed to learn a lot; not just about the art of makeup, but also about life. The person I tutored under was a very strong and independent lady and she taught me a lot.

The treatment seemed to be working fine and I was beginning to regain my health. However, at point during the treatment there was an issue that had the doctor flummoxed. Although everything seemed to be going well, there was part that was still infected and that I would need a minor surgery to have that infected area removed. I was petrified but the doctor assured me that although it was a risk, he would do his best to save the uterus. On the 18th of June, 2016, I came under the scalpel. It was for the first time that such an operation was successfully completed at Chennai Apollo Hospital. It was like I had a new lease on life and I promised to myself that I would never be lackadaisical with my health ever again and would not take any kind of risks that could lead to the removal of any of my organs.

After that day, I felt as though everything seemed so new and welcoming. I started anew with my family; my children and my husband, my business and focused mainly on my health and my career. There was a new hope for me. My husband began to be more understanding and supportive too. And with that support, in 2018, I arrived in Mumbai to further my academics. At the age of 28 I relived my lifelong dream of living the life of a student; unperturbed and undistracted by family and household responsibilities.

I came back from Mumbai and got into expanding my business while strengthening the bonds with my husband. Everything went well for a while. You could call it my karma, my destiny or sheer bad luck, my ever so husband went back to his old ways. All my requests, threats and pleas fell on deaf ears and my health took a hit again. When I consulted my doctor, he asked me a simple question that turned my life around. He asked, "Do you really love yourself?" And I found my answer right then.

That was the turning point in my life and there was a paradigm shift. I started to strongly follow the principle of "No means No" and I wouldn't settle for any kind of nonsense. Unless I saw valid reason or logic, I began to discard whatever anyone said or did. It wasn't that easy, but I persevered. There were regular fights at home and I started to feel unsafe around my husband. I would come home late and only after my husband had gone to bed. I started doing whatever I wanted or went wherever I wanted to go without informing him; leave alone taking any kind of permission. I stopped allowing him to get the upper hand and stopped obeying or cowing down to his orders or requests. In plain words, I just stopped respecting him or loving him. I started to drift into bouts of depression and also became dependent on sleeping tablets. It was like I was drifting into becoming a rebel of sorts. According to him I had lost my sanity. He also started to blame me and assassinate my character. My parents were also drawn into the ruckus that that had been created mainly because he began to threaten me with divorce if I didn't abide by his terms and conditions. I seized that opportunity to tell my parents all that had happened with me and also that they had not done me wrong.

Everyone decided that it would be best if I was referred to a psychiatrist. Based on that decision they took me to consult one in Delhi much against my wishes mainly because I knew that I had done no wrong. Not only had I done no wrong, but I knew that I wasn't insane. I knew exactly what I wanted, but everyone else felt that I wasn't being normal. I was counseled continuously for 5 days by a doctor of their choosing. In fact, there were 4 different doctors that spoke with my husband and me for the next 5 days. After they compiled their reports, they said that I was under mental trauma and that it was for no fault of mine. I broke down in the doctor's chamber that day after hearing his words. It was the cry of someone attaining freedom after a life of suffering, pain and torture. The doctor pointed out how my husband was mainly at fault and how mine was only a reaction to pain that had been bottled up for so long. They requested my husband to change his ways and that he should consider himself lucky if I were to ever come back into his life. They also advised him that should he want me back in his life, there had to be no conditions attached. They also made it crystal clear to him that he didn't have any rights over me in any way.

Chapter 2
Page 15

He finally agreed that it was because of some of his mistakes and ignorance that things became so bad. He realized and said that he would turn a new leaf and would help me as far as he possibly could and we came back to Guwahati.

I was still under restrictions because my treatment continued and was still dependent on sleeping pills to get me through the night. I would also have to attend counseling sessions 2 days a week for the next few weeks. I also had to visit the doctors in Delhi pretty regularly. I was still under heavy stress and no matter how hard I tried; I was just unable to overcome it. A few of my friends suggested that I try meditation. Based on that advice, I decided to give it a shot and enrolled for a meditation course. And I suppose that did do the trick, I was slowly weaned of the sleeping tablets and before I knew it, I was no longer dependent on them. My thinking and behavior became more stable and my anxiety levels seemed to be dropping. At the same time, I was beginning to build myself upwards, becoming more strong and confident; a new me.

I knew my options all along. I also knew that I had the rights to exercise my decisions. However, I didn't want anyone else to live a life of regret and sorrow and feel let down because of me. I was just grateful to be alive; to have found the real me and live a life of hope and positivity despite all that I had faced. In all, I had managed to come to terms with my past and look forward to a better present and future having left all that had happened behind; but not forgotten.

Maybe all the happened with me were somehow blessings in disguise because they motivated me to search for the real me. Not only did I now recognize who I was, but I had also learnt how to value, respect and love myself even more. I don't deny that I wasn't always right; I did have my share of mistakes as well. However, I also learnt that not to blame myself entirely and also give due credit for some of the harm to my husband, my in-laws and my parents. After having read all of this, I'm sure you'll agree if I say that some of the blame must also be shared with the society and some of their inane rules, customs and traditions too. After all, we are what we believe in; beliefs that are shaped right from our childhood by what we learn, experience and the kind of influencing or role models that we've had.

Chapter 2
Page 16

I don't think it was entirely my husband's fault either; our way of thinking, traits and points of view just didn't seem to be on the same wavelength. As far as I knew him, he was always very humble, well mannered, and gentle with others. In short, the opinion that I had of him was that he was a perfect gentleman. In fact, he had always been his parents' favorite child ever since his childhood.

They are originally from Tinsukia district of Upper Assam. They weren't what one can call an affluent family. His father was a teacher and they were a set of 5 siblings; 3 brothers and 2 sisters. Considering that the salary of a teacher those days wasn't really comparable to today's standards, they had to resort to earning a little extra through their farms and putting up temporary shops whenever there was an even or a fair in their neighborhood. He was the eldest among the boys and he empathized with their father's financial condition. That's why when he enrolled into a high school, he decided to take up science but refused to enroll into any extra classes which most students did at the time to score well. Despite that his focus, grit and determination got him through and he cleared with good grades. His Mahi lived in Guwahati at the time. This is the same Mahi that I spoke about earlier; the one that took up for me when I was pregnant with the first child. He always dreamt about coming to Guwahati, starting a business and settling down in the city. He enrolled into a graduation program at a college here and worked towards getting his degree with complete focus. He didn't allow any of things that most college kids indulge in to distract him. He would give private tuitions to earn his way through college in addition to taking up the responsibility of both his younger brothers. He sacrificed doing a lot of things that brought him happiness and eventually completed his graduation after which he enrolled into a law degree program and simultaneously began establishing his own business without any kind of financial help from home. As far as I know, he was so focused on establishing himself and becoming successful that he just didn't have any time for love or relationships. In about 2004, when he was 33 years old, he decided to get married and start a family and started looking for a suitable wife. That's when he met me. He had made a promise to himself that he would not even indulge in any act of love or sex till he got married.

I suppose he was right from his point of view. However, maybe I somehow couldn't match up to his idea of a perfect wife or to his desires. It could be because of the age gap between the two of us. I observed right from my childhood and have also heard of tales where many couples lived happy and content lovers despite a huge age gap between the husband and the wife. This was also evident in the case of my own parents; they lived very happily with each other despite the age difference. But I'm sure there must be some kind of exceptions and cannot be taken as a blanket rule that applies to everyone. Even when I was getting married, I was told that since he's much older, he would take good care of me, love me a lot and that he would be a lot more understanding of my needs. I believed them; partly because I had seen evidence that supported those statements and also because I was still quite naïve. Honestly, he really was very caring and understanding mostly; however there were still a few differences between the two of us, something that was natural as no two humans are ever exactly alike.

I tried my level best to match up with him, but my age itself was a major hindrance. Even in terms of physical stamina or mental strength I was no match. Also, he was a proud and rigid man; which usually most self-made people are which made the task of keeping up with him even more difficult. Perhaps it was all the responsibilities that he took and the hardships that he faced since childhood that made him what he was. Not only was he hardworking, but he was also very regimented and disciplined, things that he tried to inculcate in me too which made things all the more difficult for me. At times he would regret and apologize if he made things very difficult for me, but somehow, he would always forget and go back to being who he was.

There were times when he would use his older age and acquired experience as an advantage to prove that he was right and that I needed to comply. Maybe he was right. Nevertheless, I would still get hurt and feel sad because, at times, he would completely discount my point of view and sometimes even refuse to acknowledge it. Not only was I hurt emotionally, but I would also get physically tired because I would mostly compromise and try and do everything to try and create and maintain a healthy environment. I would try my level best to think from his point of view; in fact, I would also imagine myself to be in his age bracket and try and think things through from that perspective. This too took its toll since I got to thinking like an adult mostly; at least tried to, and as a result I didn't have anyone in my age category with whom I could share some laughs or enjoy as most teenagers would. I don't think it was very pragmatic either to have a child think like an adult; especially one that is 16 years older. Not only was it difficult for me to explain my perspective of things to my husband, but equally taxing for me was that I had to behave and think like an adult at all times. Or maybe I just wasn't trained adequately. I suppose even he didn't have things easy either, and I reckon he was hurt too somewhere down the line.

A marriage is not just an event where two people come together and promise to live together for the rest of their lives. It's also not just a union of minds and souls, but one of shared responsibilities, understanding and at times, some amount of compromise too. And to achieve that, I suppose it's very essential that the couple get to know each other better and understand each other, and to do that it's also necessary that they get to spend some time in the company of each other without the interference of any other person or social norms and diktats.

Chapter 2
Page 17

Most people take their feelings for others for granted. Many people still find it difficult to differentiate between wants and needs, love and infatuation, guilt and shame, and lust and love. Right from childhood, we are conditioned to believe that real love exists only between the family and the one you consider to be your life partner or spouse. Is that really true? If one has to be absolutely honest with the self, even in such cases, there are usually some boundaries and expectations; a very negligible one, but still there nevertheless. It's usually only when our expectations are met or when a person behaves and treats us in ways that fulfill our needs, do we actually seem to love the person. Do you think it's possible to exhibit unconditional love; a love that knows no boundaries or has no demands? Do we really practice love without any kind of strings attached? I suppose that's the most difficult stage to attain. After all we are just human, aren't we? Real and unconditional love involves a lot of patience, tolerance, lack of any expectations and the ability to forgive without any conditions or deals. That's what true spiritual love is all about. However, we as humans usually tend either never truly think about such things or just overlook all of that. And that's why we become unhappy, feel hurt, or feel let down or deceived. Even between the spouses it's difficult to exhibit pure unconditional love. There will always be some reservations; conscious or subconscious. Why is it not possible to be married without any form of social or legal stamp of authentication, or the need to procreate? Why is it that there are clashes of egos and pride, battles of dominance? Do you think such kind of relationships ever last long? Then there are those that cling on to relationships just because they're afraid of social censure. Do you think such couples can remain happy and content? There are those too who try and mould the partner to conform to their standards and their expectations resulting not just in the loss of love but also the relationship in many instances. Just because we can't get a handle on our own emotions and needs, don't we end up hurting the ones that love us the most besides hurting ourselves in the bargain? When the person that really loves us starts to do things against their wishes just to please us, don't you think that person feels hurt? Is that really love at all? Then again, don't we too feel hurt or regret our actions when we see the one we love hurt? And this just keeps on going round and round like a cycle. In that case, why is it so difficult to try and practice love without any conditions? Maybe we can, but we somehow lack the willingness to try to do so. Some people have attained that level and those who have are truly happy and content and have managed to reap the benefits of pure love. I got everything that a wife can want from a husband; commitment, money, moral support, and a lot of love. Despite all of that I still felt that there was something short, something lacking. Like I described him in an earlier part of the book; he was very well mannered, humble and behaved the perfect gentleman and like a good husband should. However, despite all the protection security that he gave me, he couldn't save me from just one thing: his own pride. I suppose, as his wife, it wasn't really out of character of him to expect a normal conjugal relationship with me. In fact, that's what most husbands would expect. But maybe, my past experience didn't allow me to behave like a normal wife would mainly because I couldn't look at sex as something good and enjoy it. Nevertheless, I have always respected him and will be ever grateful to him because if it wasn't for him perhaps I wouldn't have learnt all the things that I have today. Besides, he has treated me like a princess more often than not. In addition to all of that, he is my children's father and he leaves no shortcomings in ensuring their well being. One of the things that I've learnt is that; in a relationship, one cannot be calculative and loving at the same time and also to not just judge someone only by the hurt that they've caused but to also be grateful for the good that they've done you; to be able to take the good with the bad. Promises and commitments are just as important in a healthy relationship and perhaps there were many unkept promises in ours. There were promises that he made before we were wedded and many more after; however, many of those promises remained unfulfilled or at times, were broken. And despite making some promises when he saw me in pain, I suppose he just didn't keep them because he couldn't judge the intensity. Actions speak louder than words and they speak for themselves; is the old adage. It's very easy to make a promise. There are many times when we've made promises; and also promised never to break them, but honestly, how many of them have really been kept? It isn't always as easy as it sounds. I suppose it's also because as humans, we have a selfish streak in us right from our childhood. And that selfish trait makes us do things to get what we want, including making promises at times that we know will be difficult to keep. And that selfish streak in us remains even when we become parents. Many us try and fulfill our broken dreams through our children. Our selfishness expects that our children will take care of us once we're old and incapable of looking after ourselves. And even if that isn't on your mind, I'm sure every parent will expect that their children will at least come to see them off when they leave this life. We expect our children to do things that will make us feel proud and maybe even show them off to others just to raise our own worth or self esteem. We expect our children to follow and obey us at all times including allowing us to choose who they should wed and when. Most couples also tie the knot with the selfish expectation of fulfilling their dreams with the spouse. Each one expects the other to share the same dreams, goals, and ambitions. Each one expects the other to be or behave the way they'd like them to be. In many societies, including this one, he husband expects the wife to obey his commands, conform to his needs, fulfill his sexual desires and remain a true partner through his life among many other things. In essence; in varying degrees, we are self centered and we expect others; especially the ones we love, to fulfill our desires. And when that person fails to deliver or meet up to our expectations, we find it difficult to accept and admit our shortcomings. A relationship isn't built just on a tag or social acceptance; it's a matter of the heart that needs to be nurtured with a lot of love, care and affection. Perhaps I didn't receive the kind of mental and moral support that I expected from either my parents or my husband. And much to my dismay, maybe my husband was a little too rigid in his beliefs, which eventually surpassed my limits of tolerance.

Let's just assume that no one or nothing is to be blamed; not the predators who tried to exploit me as a child, not my parents' decision to marry me off so early, not my husband, or not even myself. One thing however, is for sure. The things that make up our emotions and affect the way we think are an accumulation of the experiences that we've had since our childhood and the people that have influenced us along the way. In addition to all of that, the kind of society that we are raised in, the cultural or traditional practices that we are exposed to also play a major role in shaping us and making us who we are. And then there are the other factors like the intelligence quotient, emotional quotient and the ability to innovate and create that can make the individual who they are; someone with a lot of positivity and optimism, or one filled with pessimism and negativity.

No one is born evil or wanting to be evil. No one wants to willingly do things that can hurt others. Likewise, no one in their right senses ties the knot wanting to destroy their spouse's life. But then, there are times when there's a definite mismatch which is found only much later. And this is exactly what may have happened in our case. Maybe my husband wasn't what I dreamt about and I suppose, I wasn't the kind of woman that my husband thought about marrying. I reckon we had different goals, different dreams and different sets of principles and ways of looking at life. I may have found it very difficult to accept my husband the way he is because of the incidents that happened with me during my childhood. Also, getting married so early in life without a proper understanding of the life; mainly marital life may have played a major role in causing a sense of discord; especially after a sense of realization dawned on me. Like I mentioned in the earlier pages, I was too young to know anything and blindly obeyed my elders' orders unquestioningly like I was taught to do. Besides the difference in our outlook to life, our ego clashes also created a lot of friction in the relationship. In one of the earlier chapters I had described how my father would also bring home in criminals who had been set free after their terms. Maybe that environment taught me that criminals are no different from any other person and that they need to be treated with love and affection too. And that's why I overlooked some of the harm that my husband caused me thinking that they were absolutely normal things to do. Since I couldn't really tell what a crime was or who a criminal is, I suppose I started becoming the victim at all times. In fact, I always thought that I was the bad one; the criminal, especially when all fingers pointed at me when I tried to end it all. But yes, those were some of the worst days of my life when I was physically hurt, mentally disturbed and emotionally shattered. What made things worse is that I considered it a great sin to have even allowed the thought that I didn't love my husband to cross my mind. Why? Because the society that I came from and the way I was raised always taught me that a husband is an equivalent of God and it's one of the greatest sins to think about not loving one's husband. It was like I knew what was right and wrong and at the same time knew nothing at all.

If I look at it from my husband's perspective; the place where he was raised and the environment that he grew up in, perhaps there were no similarities with mine. He was raised in an environment where the man of the house is considered to be supreme and that he needs to be commanding and have the ability to hold the home together at all times. His rigidity and unwillingness to compromise did hurt me to a great extent. But that doesn't mean that he was a bad person. It was his upbringing, the way he was groomed and conditioned since childhood. Perhaps he didn't have anyone who could have actually guided him; explained to him the right way and the incorrect way to treat a wife and how to maintain a happy, content, and most of all, loving marital life. I believe that love doesn't necessarily always have to result in sex and sex doesn't always mean that you love the person. And a conjugal relationship is healthy only when it's mutual; and if even one of the partners is unwilling, and other ignore and insists, it becomes an offence. There are many other ways to display love.

earlier chapters I had described how my father would also bring home in criminals who had been set free after their terms. Maybe that environment taught me that criminals are no different from any other person and that they need to be treated with love and affection too. And that's why I overlooked some of the harm that my husband caused me thinking that they were absolutely normal things to do. Since I couldn't really tell what a crime was or who a criminal is, I suppose I started becoming the victim at all times. In fact, I always thought that I was the bad one; the criminal, especially when all fingers pointed at me when I tried to end it all. But yes, those were some of the worst days of my life when I was physically hurt, mentally disturbed and emotionally shattered. What made things worse is that I considered it a great sin to have even allowed the thought that I didn't love my husband to cross my mind. Why? Because the society that I came from and the way I was raised always taught me that a husband is an equivalent of God and it's one of the greatest sins to think about not loving one's husband. It was like I knew what was right and wrong and at the same time knew nothing at all.

If I look at it from my husband's perspective; the place where he was raised and the environment that he grew up in, perhaps there were no similarities with mine. He was raised in an environment where the man of the house is considered to be supreme and that he needs to be commanding and have the ability to hold the home together at all times. His rigidity and unwillingness to compromise did hurt me to a great extent. But that doesn't mean that he was a bad person. It was his upbringing, the way he was groomed and conditioned since childhood. Perhaps he didn't have anyone who could have actually guided him; explained to him the right way and the incorrect way to treat a wife and how to maintain a happy, content, and most of all, loving marital life. I believe that love doesn't necessarily always have to result in sex and sex doesn't always mean that you love the person. And a conjugal relationship is healthy only when it's mutual; and if even one of the partners is unwilling, and other ignore and insists, it becomes an offence. There are many other ways to display love.

Chapter 2
Page 18

The way we think, behave and treat others; in fact, what we are as adults and our overall outlook towards life is shaped right from our childhood. That's because memories never die; they may be relegated to our subconscious mind, but they can never be deleted. That's why the way we raise our children, how we treat them, how we protect them is very important; just so they have a brighter and better future.

Many of our misdeeds; even the ones we commit unknowingly, influence children in a very negative way. They tend to observe everything we do and say and tend to copy them. And if they figure out that the deed isn't really socially acceptable, they tend to do it behind the parents' backs. And this usually carries forward to their adult life. In case a child notices an adult doing or saying something that the child is not supposed to be exposed to, it is very important; as a responsible adult, to sit the child down and explain what it was all about in the simplest possible way and to also tell the child how the thing that they saw or heard can be harmful. Unless we do that, it can influence the child in a very negative way; either the child will repeat the action thinking that it's the right thing to do, or the child could be left absolutely confused and clueless. In fact, there's every possibility that the child will develop some kind of an apprehension against the adults they trust. Not only is it important to check one's behavior and attitude after the child is born. There is; in fact, growing evidence that many children learn things right from the time they're in the womb. This has also been mentioned in the Mahabharata where Arjun's son Abhimanyu begins to learn how to break into a particular battle formation called the "Chakravayu". As per the tale, Abhimanyu learns how to break into the formation while he was still in the womb, however, owing to certain circumstances, didn't get to learn how to exit. As the tale goes, in the war of Kurukshetra, Abhimanyu managed to infiltrate the Chakravayu formation that the enemy had built; but since he didn't learn how to get out, he was trapped and finally killed. The point I'm trying to make is that a mother-to-be needs to take good care of herself at least for the sake of the child in the womb. And by this, I don't mean it in just the physical sense; but equally important is that she takes care of herself emotionally and mentally. She needs to remain exposed to peaceful surroundings, read good books, and surround herself and the little one in as much positivity as possible. And this is not just essential for the well being of the mother-to-be, but is equally important for the unborn child as it will carry a major part of that influence throughout its life.

History teaches us many things. However, most people tend to ignore the events or the teachings. As they say, "Those that don't know their history are bound to repeat it." Hence many people tend to make the same mistakes as others have done before them. And unless we know our history well enough, it will be difficult to change ourselves and in society which could make this a better world to live in. And since children are the future, it's very important that they understand the world better so that they can analyze and learn to create a better world for themselves. It's very important that they learn the principle of "Who, What, How, and Why; so that they can better implement what they learn. Since it is parents that play the most important role in their formative years, it's very important that parents guide their children through proper logic and reason instead of just imposing laws on to them which may make no sense to the child after a while. There are times when a child's future is dulled just because the parents neglect explaining things properly or were too rigid which automatically allowed the child to abuse freedom once it reached adulthood.

Because of what happened to me in my childhood, I spent the first part of my life; the foundation, in fear. The next phase of my life I spent in fear of society induced depression mainly because I was married off before I came into and age of understanding. All the added responsibilities and my state of mind finally; in desperation, led me to take the extreme step of hurting myself physically. I couldn't tell anyone anything although I knew that I was being wronged. I obeyed everyone and couldn't refuse anything although I knew I was harming myself just because they were all elder to me. Practicing patience to me was like I was playing a solo game with my emotional and mental state. All this just because I was taught to respect and obey my elders and also led to believe that they were more experienced and always knew what was best for me. I was always told that parents should always be respected and that my husband would never do anything to hurt me. Not just me, but this is what is generally told to almost all women across the country which does; at some point in time, have a negative effect on many women.

And in between all of this, who was affected along with me? It was my children; especially the first born because the days he was in the womb were some of the worst days of my life; days where I was under tremendous stress and was constantly depressed. There are many times when; consciously or unconsciously, we pass on a lot of our negative traits and thinking to the next generation. Just like it's next to impossible to uproot a tree that has dug its roots deep into the ground, the characteristics that we instill into a child just keeps growing deeper and deeper till at one point in time it becomes very difficult to get rid of some of the traits. That's why it's very important to nurture a child very carefully. The acquired experiences and knowledge will set the platform for how the child will behave once it becomes an adult. And these characteristics will pass on to the succeeding generations. In case the experiences and the knowledge gathered is inclined more towards negativity and destruction, chances are that the future generations will continue down the same path and likewise if the experiences and knowledge gathered tilts towards a positive and constructive outlook.

Many people spend many stressful years running to a court of law even though they know that they are in the right. Why? Only because they need that stamped approval saying that they're right. In fact, even the wrong doer knows that a crime or a wrong has been committed; so does the victim. Yet they still slug it out in a court of law just to prove that the self to be right. There are many instances where even the one that has committed the crime is proved to be innocent or in the right, and in such cases the actual victim gives up the fight thinking that there's no justice. In such cases it's the victim that suffers the most. There are examples of women that kill themselves because of dowry issues, and many suffer silently despite being in the right knowing that society and its rules have wronged them. Many girls have died just because their parents decided or chose wrongly. More often than not people regret the mistakes only after it's too late; after the girl is dead or maimed for life, and apologize. But just a sorry doesn't bring back one from the dead or return what has been lost. Instead, why not just nip it in the bud and protect that girl from harm? When I realized that I had been wronged and harmed at the same time, I could have filed a case which; in all probabilities, have been in my favor. But, to what end? If I would have stuck by my rights only and walked out of the marriage, the one who would have suffered the most for no fault of theirs would have been my children. When deep within I already knew where I was right and where I was wrong, if I would have taken that decision, I would have been the fool. That's because I already knew the truth and I knew I wasn't in the wrong, and I didn't really need the authentication of a court or society.

Instead of fighting and regretting the decision later, wouldn't it just be easier to change and stop allowing the self to be wronged and mistreated by taking stringent measures and setting strict boundaries? After one has been hurt and wronged, is it possible to erase the mistakes of the past and mend a relationship with just a few apologies? I'm sure you'll agree that it isn't really possible to delete memories, especially the ones that leave scars. Instead, why not then create a general sense of awareness for a better society and better future?

I was labeled foolish and psychotic. Why? Was it just because I rebelled and stopped blindly obeying inane rules and began to point out things that I thought were wrong after I realized what had been happening to me all the while? Was it only because I could no longer tolerate the injustice that I felt and stopped acting like the sacrificial lamb? Did people begin to doubt me just because I stopped obeying my husband's commands and refused to acquiesce to his demands? The fact of the matter is that everyone; including my husband, had gotten so used to my compliance to their requests and demands that they never thought that I could or would ever react or go against their wishes. But no one actually tried to sit down, talk to me, or even try and understand what I was going through. It seemed no one even made a feeble attempt at actually trying to figure out why I reacted in such a way after years of being so docile and submissive. Maybe no one really cared. There are many women in our country, in society, who are, till date scared of disobeying their husbands just because they lack the financial and social support that is needed. But such women also need to realize that if they remain silent despite the injustice that is being meted out to them, then they are equally at fault. I reacted to the injustice when the realization dawned on me; however, for my husband, I was only being foolish and nonsensical because of which he dragged me for counseling. No one however thought to try and understand that even I was a living person and that even I had my own needs, wants, dreams and ambitions; which were my basic rights. In fact, even my parents asked me to calm down and tolerate all that was going on because they were scared and worried of what the future might hold for me and my children. They were scared that there would be no one to look after me or my children if I continued the way I did. In a nutshell, I lacked the kind of support that I expected even from my parents. And this lack of understanding and support is not just specific to the Indian subcontinent or Indian culture, but is prominent in many other countries and cultures around the globe. In that case who is really at fault? Is it logical or pragmatic to remain silent and tolerate all the injustice? And if we do that, aren't we committing a major crime? Aren't we being criminals ourselves, with the self being the victim too?

Chapter 2
Page 19

The word "Society" is a lot more than a just a string of letters put together. The Oxford Dictionary defines it to be "The aggregate of people living together in a more or less ordered community", or "a community of people living in a particular country or region and having shared customs, laws and organizations". In both the definitions and all the others that follow, it just proves that a society is normally built on shared love and respect for each other, to protect one another and to help progress develop as a whole. After all, man is a social animal and mostly cannot survive in isolation. We are born into, live in and eventually die in a society. Through our lifetimes, we derive a lot from the society that we're in: education, knowledge, culture, traditions, and behaviors. The society that we live in also has a profound effect on the way we dress, the way we speak and even the way we treat others. In fact, almost all the laws of the land are also derived from the socially accepted norms of that region; and most of the laws are designed to protect the people that form that society and also help the populace progress and develop.

But then again, some of the laws; written, verbal, or in some cases, just accepted, can be detrimental too. There are times when rules and laws are based simply on fear and lack of adequate knowledge. These are the ones that can harm quite a few people of that society; willingly or unwillingly. One of the examples is when a new bride enters her marital home she has to face many situations and norms that may be alien to her at first because there are bound to be a few differences in the cultural values between the bride and the groom's families. However, she's constantly judged by the way she behaves and the way she dresses. Instead of welcoming her and making her feel at home and easing her into a new way of life, she's expected to undergo a complete change in her lifestyle very rapidly. Isn't that in a way the fault of the society that she's come into after being married? Why do many families choose to showcase their traditional or cultural values only through the bride? Why most families are so overtly concerned with how the new bride dresses; conventionally and traditionally, instead of finding out if she's comfortable is indeed baffling. Instead of being rigid about customs and traditions which may eventually lead to the falling out of the relationship, isn't it better to just try and understand the new bride and ease her into things just so that she's comfortable and help her build a relationship with the family? It does lead to a harassment of sorts to force the bride to wear what she's uncomfortable in just in the name of cultural or traditional values. After all, the bride gets married and enters the new home expecting that she'll be loved and respected for what she is and not just what she wears. Yet, the focus is mostly on the way she dresses. In between all of this, I would like to know if everyone really abides by all that the customs and traditions that have been laid down. It doesn't seem likely, however, the new bride is definitely made to live by them just so that the in-laws can prove their superiority and have the upper hand.

What do most people expect out of their children? I suppose every parent wants their children to be well educated, financially settled and lead a dignified life in a dignified society. There are also parents that push their children to be super achievers; be it in academic or professional careers. Whatever the case, almost all parents want that their children become a pillar of support for them towards the dusk of their lives. At the same time, most parents; especially of the Indian subcontinent, also prefer that their children marry someone of their parents' choosing; someone from the same community, religion, or caste. Why is that so? Is it just so that the parents can show off how well they have raised their children? Is it just so that they can continue to receive approval from the society that they live in? However, at the end of it all, who do you think is going to outlast the parents? Who do you think is going to have to live with a choice that was primarily the parents' and not their own? Isn't that tantamount to being selfish on the part of the parents? Is the fulfillment of one's dreams the main reason behind giving birth to children? Can we call it unconditional love when we mould and manipulate our children to do our bidding, fulfill our dreams and not give them the space to grow, develop and live their lives as they wish? I suppose this sort of behavior holds true for almost all parents barring a few exceptions where the parents actually allow the children to take their own decisions.

Why do we hurt our children just so that we can achieve our own selfish objectives; so that we can live our dreams through them? No child signs any kind of agreement stating that they will live their lives exactly according to their parents' wishes, do they? Or do they make any commitments after they're born that they'll do exactly what we parents desire? But from the time they come to an age of understanding, we parents inculcate some habits and traits in them that; no matter how hard they try, they can't rid themselves of them. Sometimes, we parents also unknowingly condition them in a way that can be detrimental to them and hinder their progress in life. For example, although humility is considered to be a virtue, being too humble and the lack of aggression can be considered a hindrance and some circumstances and can cause it to be a hurdle in the child's progress. There are also times when the child knows what they've learnt doesn't apply to them anymore, however, they're afraid to implement what's right and practical just because it has been ingrained in them not to hurt their parents or go against society norms just so that they don't feel ostracized. There are also many times when people suffer just because of a few inane laws and rules that society imposes on them. And just because the person doesn't conform to what society expects them to do, they become the topic of gossip, their characters assassinated, and sometimes even ostracized. This behavior has led to many becoming depressed, mentally ill or suicidal. And this is especially true for women for they suffer the most when they decide to do things that they like which may not be socially acceptable. But is society actually right in doing so? Does a woman have to be treated with contempt and looked down upon when she doesn't mean to hurt anyone and only does the things that make her happy? Is it right to physically or emotionally abuse her just because she doesn't want to abide by some customs or traditions that she doesn't find any logic in? And most women that are dependent on the society that they live in continue to suffer silently; especially in a country like India, just because they're scared to revolt against the system or speak up for their rights for fear of social criticism and abuse. Or maybe we women are at fault ourselves for bringing ourselves to this predicament mainly because we become so dependent and fear the society that we live in that we decide to compromise and sacrifice our values and beliefs and eventually lose our true selves; break that relationship with ourselves. Just to conform to some of societies inane beliefs and just so that we receive constant approval, we end up committing a huge crime; a crime against ourselves.

Yes, it's very imperative to graduate from a renowned school with good grades in this century if one wants to progress professionally. However, equally important for personal advancement is the knowledge of one's basic rights, methods to protect oneself from physical, mental and sexual abuse. It's equally important to develop self confidence and self esteem so that one need not ever feel less than anyone else. And this is especially true for women mainly so that social evils like child abuse, child marriage and unwanted early pregnancies can be thwarted. And unless we do this, such social evils will continue to exist and so will physical, emotional and mental violence against women. And without a healthy woman population the country may continue to progress; however sans any real development.

Besides my father's advice on my marriage day about women being like water and not carrying any gossip about the in-law's place for a happy and content married life, I had heard many other things. Among some of the other things that I heard from my childhood were that a woman's corpse, once married, will only leave from the husband's home and that no matter what, a wife must always stick by her husband and no matter what must never leave him. I believed most of them to be universal truths and tried my level best to live by those principles. I tried to be fluid like water and fit into every situation and almost forgot myself in the bargain. I didn't gossip and kept quiet no matter how hurt I was and eventually became the victim because I couldn't seek guidance from anyone. And just because I believed that I should be by my husband and never leave him no matter what, I overlooked all the bad in him.

I suppose my biggest drawback was that I obeyed everyone's advice without a real understanding of when and how to apply them. The result was that I harmed myself more with that little knowledge that I had. No advice is actually bad or intended to cause any harm, however, it's also equally important to teach the person or the one receiving the advice on how and when to apply them. However, many of us dish out advice, sometimes without even properly understanding the implications. As the adage goes, "A little knowledge is a dangerous thing", so it's very important that we have an in-depth knowledge of the situation and the person before dishing out any kind of advice, lest that advice does more harm than good.

Through this book, I wish to request all parents, educators and society at large to begin teaching our children to differentiate between a "Good Touch" and a "Bad Touch" and also how to protect themselves from sex predators. Even if the school or he learning center lacks the facilities, I would request all the people that run such centers to avoid procrastinating such teachings and improvise in the best possible manner. Your initiative could save quite a few children and hence future generations from turning into degenerated beings suffering from depression related issues and a general fear and disgust of society. Not just the authorities or the government, it is our duty individually too to remain vigilant and aware and create an atmosphere that is protective towards all our children; including the ones on the streets, and conducive to their overall development. It's also important that we stop or deter people from marrying off young girls forcibly even when they turn 18; the legal age for marriage. There are still many instances where girls who've turned 18 are forcibly married off for reasons best known to the parents.

However, just because the girl has turned 18 doesn't necessarily mean that she's mature enough and ready to shoulder the heavy responsibilities of a household. The worst part is that even though legally accepted, in many cases the girl doesn't attain complete physical, mental and emotional maturity. Even worse is that in most cases it is noticed that the girl is given no choice and is married off; either by force, coercion or manipulation, without her consent or without her even knowing what she's getting into.

Keep our children safe, let them blossom into the beautiful human beings that they are meant to grow up to be, let them know real happiness and let's not spoil their lives just so that we can live our dreams, fulfill our lust or just so that we can be happy is the only request that I make to all you readers and society at large through this book.

Life is beautiful and that beauty needs to be explored and experienced. Please don't allow your needs and wants to take advantage of others, least of all innocent little children, and cause them harm; knowingly or unknowingly. Happiness derived from others' pain isn't real happiness. And this is mentioned in almost all books, sayings and stories that deal with human values. In fact, there is no system in the world that teaches us to be happy by harming others.

*You may be wondering what my life is like at present. After all that I've been through, all the hurt, abuse and the mental trauma that I've lived through. Is there a possibility of me living a normal; emotionally, mentally, and physically healthy life? The answer to all of that is a definite "Yes". I can very safely say that I live a perfectly normal life today, just like most other people do. I won't deny that there are the daily challenges that do get to me at times, however, it has nothing to do with the past life. These are challenges that almost everyone encounters on a day-to-day basis; from a burnt toast to a flat tire to financial issues, life goes on as usual. And how has all that been possible? That's mainly because I don't regret all that I've done, and neither do I hold on to the past. Yes, I have learnt from the past no doubt, however, to me, it makes absolutely no sense whatsoever holding on to grudges. That's just additional baggage that I refuse to carry today. Most of all, I don't regret the decisions that I made and that actions that I took just to behave according to societal demands. It's a possibility that my children would've had more of a normal and secure upbringing had I lived according to the norms accepted by my parents and society at large, and kept my mouth shut and maintained the appearances of a peaceful, happy married life against my innermost desires. It did take me a lot of soul searching and questioning my motives. I asked myself if I was truly happy now or would I have been happier in a marriage that was forced onto me, would I have been more at peace with myself living what I believed is right or should I have gone along with the norms set by society? In both cases, I strongly believe that my choices made me a better person and more so, a person who my innermost self can look up to, love and respect. I no longer need to pop pills to climb into bed and go to sleep. I no longer have to lay awake through the night in fear; fear that I will be taken advantage of. In fact, more often than not, I enjoy a nice healthy sleep whenever I do. Just 32 years of my life seems to have taught me a lot. What I've learnt is that unless I think about myself, unless I learnt how to be responsible for myself; and unless I learn how to love myself, no one is going to understand me. If I'm to expect people to understand and respect me for who I am, I need to first know myself well; identify my likes and dislikes, what hurts me and what doesn't, and behave and act accordingly. My first experience with Vipassana meditation technique was in 2018. My turning point was when I got back from that first Vipassana mediation retreat. It was for the first time that I could go to bed and sleep peacefully without popping any sleeping pills or using marijuana. It's one of those moments in my life that I just can't forget. In fact, the first thing that I did after I got back from the retreat was fulfil a long-time dream. Yes, I participated in a beauty pageant. I began to focus on my health and my academics. It's not that I made progress in leaps and strides, however, what I noticed was that the progress was consistent and most of all, I was no longer fearful. I stopped fearing the repercussions of not living according to my husband's wishes and demands. I was no longer fearful of rejecting his sexual advances. I stopped thinking about what society would think about me and how it would accept me in case my husband decided to legally separate; something that he would frequently threaten me with. These were things that were constantly on my mind before I went into the retreat, however, they no longer held true. I was the loneliest during the most disturbing times of my life. I always yearned to tell someone my innermost fears, find someone to confide in, someone who'd understand me and offer me some solace or at least an empathetic hearing. Things just got worse when I could find no such person and I went into an even darker place in my mind; became almost traumatic. I tried to escape and looked for solace in alcohol, weed and parties. I had become habituated to substance and continuously looked for a way out. I thought about chucking it all away; break all relationships, abstain from all responsibilities, run away and live by myself. There were times when I would contemplate getting into a meditation centre with the hope that that might work for me. But I was confused between which would be the better option; meditation, or running away. During the worst phase of my mental imbalance which was in 2018, I started to travel a lot, went trekking, started observing fasting periods where I would abstain from eating anything, avoided crowds and started to cut myself off from all the people that I knew. Seeing my behaviour then, my husband and my brother decided to take me to the best psychiatrist in the country that they could think off, and they did. After a whole lot of therapy and counselling sessions, the counsellors advised my husband not to force me into doing things anymore and to allow me to live my life the way I thought best (All this has been explained in detail in an earlier chapter in the book). Things took a turn for the worse though. I started to skip the counselling sessions and started depending on sleeping tablets. Things came to such that I smoke a joint after popping a sleeping pill just to ensure that I slept through the night and not wake up in between; which was something I dreaded. I was always fearful that I would wake up in the middle of the night and not be able to go back to sleep. It was during this time that a friend of mine first suggested that I try Vipassana. The second time another friend suggested the same thing was when I was on trek. Two instances and the same suggestion had me interested. What actually interested me more was that going into a Vipassana retreat would allow me to remain cut off from people, stay away from all relationships and abstain from my responsibilities; something that I had been wanting anyway. Plans were made on the spur of the moment and I left for Kolkatta to get into a Vipassana retreat. There were certain rules that one needs to follow while at a Vipassana retreat. Of the five precepts of Vipassana, one also needs to remain abstinent from any intoxicants. However, here I was, at the retreat; something that I had been yearning for, but I was still popping antidepressants. I remember the day very clearly. It was the 3rd day of meditation and Pallavi, who was a friend of mine and at the retreat with me, broke her vow of "Noble Silence" only to request me to try and give up the pill for at least a day. She was the only one who was aware that I was still popping pills. Since she had risked her stay at the retreat by breaking her vow of "Noble Silence", I decided that I must respect her attempt at helping me for my own benefit, and I must try and stay without the pill; at least for her sake. She was one of the older meditators who had been practicing the form for quite a while and she exuded a string aura around her. That night I went to bed without the pill and eventually fell asleep while meditating. The next morning was one of the most amazing mornings of my life. I actually woke up without any feeling of anxiety or fear and felt absolutely refreshed and like I had made a new beginning. I could actually enjoy the sunrise and be at peace with myself. For those not familiar with the ways of Vipassana meditation, "Noble Silence" is a vow that one must take before entering the retreat where one is not allowed to communicate with other members either verbally or non-verbally; which also includes reading and writing. For those who've never tried it, it is one of the toughest forms of meditation. Eventually, I got into the habit of meditating and begun to find relief from many of my worries. I changed, I began to look at things in more positive light and sense of realisation dawned on me. I began to understand how I had been wrong on many counts. And one of those realisations was how I had wrongly classified all men. I began to become more emotionally and mentally stable and began to connect with men without fear. I began to rid myself of the prejudices that I held against men and started looking at them in newer light. I began to understand that not all men are the same and that even they are able to maintain healthy relationships without any sexual connotations. I have to admit. Meditation for me was like being reborn into a new life. I still have my share of ups and downs. After all, isn't that what life is all about? However, yes, I have made a lot of progress and come far away from that torturous world that I was living in. There are still times when I feel helpless and lonely however, that doesn't turn me into a depressive state anymore. That's because I have no regrets about my past life anymore. 30 odd years of living have taught me a lot and I know that there's still a lot more to learn. The only thing that I feel is certain at this point in time is that whatever else I'm yet to learn will be more connected to positivity. There are still tough situations that I face now and then, however, the main difference is that such situations do not bring about panic or anxiety attacks any longer. In 2019, I decided that it was time for me to fulfil my dreams and aspirations that I had been neglecting for so long. Dreams that I had given up on since I found no support. I started studying again and working on re-developing some of my skill sets. It didn't matter how long it took, but I needed to give it my best and at least try so that I could look up to myself in the future and perhaps even inspire my children later on in life. Then came the pandemic in 2020 that affected many lives adversely. However, this period turned out to be a blessing in disguise for me. It provided me with an opportunity to mend my relationship with my husband; a relationship that I thought had broken beyond repair. It gave us the opportunity to build a healthy and friendly relationship once again. It was only obvious that there would have been some friction between us. After all, I decided to start living my way; something that my husband found very difficult to digest. He could never fathom the idea of me reacting to all those incidents the way I did and how I found my sense of independence at the end of it all. Since 2005, I had given up living for the things that I liked; that I dreamt about, and lived only according to my husband's likes and dislikes. Yes, we are going in for a divorce now. But, at least it's all happening through a whole lot of mutual understanding. But I must mention something here about my husband's supportive nature or perhaps his love towards me that he helped me to get this book written. And I must also admit that though he had hurt me either knowingly or unknowingly, he neutralized it by realizing his mistakes and apologizing to me for everything. However, there are times when our egos clash. And when that happens, the decisions we take also affects the fulfillment of our responsibilities towards the kids. However, I still try and look at things in positive light. As a mother, I may not be able to give them all the happiness that they look for, or even all the materialistic things that most children their age yearn for. One thing I'm certain of is that, I can at least help them to grow up to be mentally and emotionally healthy and strong adults. I sternly object to society's view that children of divorced parents are always affected adversely and tend to go astray. My point of view also involves the children of those parents who seemingly live a normal life and maintain a healthy relationship among themselves. There are times when children even from such families don't turn out the way people expected them to and live lives that aren't completely in tune with societal norms. I myself am one such example. My parents had a perfectly normal relationship and still do, however, look at what I had to go through and what had become of me; sad, depressed and lonely for a very long time of the prime of my life. I know that there are many out there who aren't and will not be very supportive of this decision to separate from my husband. Does that actually bog me down? No, it doesn't. Because, through the darkest moments of my life, there was no one who came to me to offering any kind of solace. I was all alone and had to fight all those battles on my own. What I've learnt through all of my life's experiences is that all philosophers and spiritual people were right when they said that we come into this world alone and we leave this world alone. I've also come to understand and believe that it is the tough times in our lives that help us grow stringer spiritually and mentally and prepares us to face all challenges peacefully. It's always better to accept the darkness of the past and move on rather than living in that past in sorrow, regret, resentments and dejection; to leave the past behind and move on to better one's today so that the future can be brighter. After all, our lives are limited and we must all move on some day or the other. It makes no sense to carry our regrets, sorrows and resentments to the final destination; rather it's about living life to its fullest and leaving this world happy, content and with a smile on the face. It's better to focus on the things that we can do and trying to achieve those to the best of our abilities instead of living in a world of lost dreams. It is said that time heals all wounds. However, there are some wounds that were so deep that the scars refuse to go. And that's just how it is with me too. There are times when the memories from the past come back to haunt me no matter how hard I try to not remember and not give it any importance. However, I work around that by focusing on my today; staying positive, doing what's at hand and not getting involved in petty gossip. For me, it's the today that matters the most and I prefer living in my today rather than the darkness of the past or the uncertainty of the future. That's mainly because I know now that I can't change the past, however, I can take care of my today in an attempt to have a better future. I am really grateful for this life. And the one thing that keeps me motivated is if I don't better my today and try and do something that benefit the future generations, how is my life any different from others'? If I don't do the things that I'm supposed to do for myself and the next generation, how do I express gratitude for the life that I have now? I sincerely believe that if I strive every day to contribute something towards society; no matter how small or how insignificant, to try and make this world a better place for the future generations, only then will I have served my purpose in life and made it worth the while. Living in a world of self-pity, blaming others, only sharing what went wrong with my life in search for sympathy seem to be a complete waste of time for me and not really worth it. I sincerely believe that there are problems and there are solutions to those problems. I trust more in living in the solutions instead of dwelling in the problems. No one can understand one another completely. No one can feel the pain that the other is going through. The only thing one can do is visualize the situation and imagine what it could be like. That's it. No two people are alike or think the same way. Likewise, neither is pain. There can only be similarities, however, there are bound to be some differences. Keeping that in mind, how is anyone supposed to be able to help anyone else overcome their pain, or how is anyone supposed to be able to guide a person in suffering? Each one to her/himself and each one needs to take steps to help the self instead of relying on others. One needs to learn how to love the self; something that I have. I have learnt how to love myself for who I am and that's why I try not to do the things that cause me harm. Instead, I am determined to do all that I can keep myself joyful, motivated and vibrant. Like almost any other girl, I too had dreams. I too wanted to have friends, live a more independent life with not too many unnecessary restrictions. However, life doesn't always happen the way you want it to and such was my case too. One thing is for certain though, today I try my best to fulfill whatever dreams I once had. Despite all the positivity mixed with a busy schedule, there are times when a sense of loneliness creeps in. After all, I am human. There are times when I feel exhausted; mentally, physically and emotionally. But then again, the challenges and the excitement of starting a new life helps me get back on my feet and I get going once again. Like I mentioned earlier, I've learnt to let go and don't hold on to the past. Right from my childhood, I had always wanted to walk the ramp and be associated with the silver screen and also try to do something worthwhile for society specially to try and help the underprivileged or the deprived. And I'm living that dream now, by keeping myself busy most of the time, getting involved in whatever work comes up and doing what's in front of me. I keep reminding myself that I can keep others happy and contribute something to society only if I can keep myself happy and content by living life on my terms and doing the things that bring me joy and satisfaction. In 2018 I participated in a beauty pageant for the very first time; something that was a lifelong dream. Yes! I was scared stiff. After all, I had no experience whatsoever and neither did I have anyone to guide me through the process or train me. Nevertheless, I was absolutely satisfied with just the fact that I at least managed to fulfill one of my lifelong dreams. I also took up a small role in a movie after a long time. Standing in front of the camera after eons at least helped regain a lot of my lost confidence. I'm also involved with a few orphanages and societies that help the underprivileged and try and help out the best way I can despite whatever limitation I might have. There are times when I come across children and, sometimes even adults, who tell me about their struggles and how they wished that they could have attained some form of formal education and how they were deprived because of their socio-economic conditions. I hear such stories and their regrets and mostly end up empathizing with them. There are many out there who just give up and resign to their fate while some actually decide to end it all and try and find relief by committing suicide. I actually feel their pain and anguish since I have been down that path and that's why I try and help such people out as far as I can. Even if I am unable to offer financial assistance, I try my best by helping out in the best way I can. At times, it's just an empathetic ear and sometimes just a nudge in the right direction that leads them out of that darkness towards a life of contentment and joy. I suppose that's how I manage to express my gratitude to an unseen God or to that energy out there that has been guiding for so long. I'm not sure how successful I will be at the end of it all. All I have to fall back on is hope and whole lot of positive energy and that's all I use to forge ahead. The past is gone; and so is the energy of my youth. That doesn't mean I use that as an excuse to deter me from doing what needs to be done to better my today and eventually my future. I choose not to spend my today and the future in self-pity and regret because I know for a fact that I can do nothing to alter the past. I also know that living in the past will only worsen my future and sincerely believe that being steadfastly courageous combined with a positive attitude will always take me to a brighter place.

The thing that I've learnt is that there is no real sadness or happiness, darkness or light. It all depends on how we look at things and how we accept the situations around us. The game is all about accepting the situation as it is, figuring out how to come out of it in a peaceful and serene way, holding on to that hope that things can get better and then taking the requisite action.*

www.ingramcontent.com/pod-product-compliance
Ingram Content Group UK Ltd.
Pitfield, Milton Keynes, MK11 3LW, UK
UKHW022235230426
12048UKWH00018BA/1270